AMERICANS
THE *Spirit* OF A *Nation*

JESSE JAMES

"I Will Never Surrender"

Jeff Burlingame

Enslow Publishers, Inc.
40 Industrial Road
Box 398
Berkeley Heights, NJ 07922
USA

http://www.enslow.com

Library of Congress Cataloging-in-Publication Data

Burlingame, Jeff.
  Jesse James : "I will never surrender" / Jeff Burlingame.
    p. cm. — (Americans—the spirit of a nation)
    Includes bibliographical references and index.
    Summary: "Discusses the life of Jesse James, including his childhood, the James-Younger gang, the many robberies he committed, his murder, and his legacy in American history"—Provided by publisher.
  ISBN-13: 978-0-7660-3353-5
  ISBN-10: 0-7660-3353-8
    1. James, Jesse, 1847–1882—Juvenile literature. 2. Outlaws—West (U.S.)—Biography—Juvenile literature. 3. Frontier and pioneer life—West (U.S.)—Juvenile literature. 4. West (U.S.)—History—1860–1890—Juvenile literature. 5. West (U.S.)—Biography—Juvenile literature. I. Title.
  F594.J27B87 2009
  364.15'52092—dc22
  [B]
                                    2008048699

Printed in the United States of America

092009 Lake Book Manufacturing, Inc., Melrose Park, IL

10 9 8 7 6 5 4 3 2 1

To Our Readers:
We have done our best to make sure all Internet Addresses in this book were active and appropriate when we went to press. However, the author and the publisher have no control over and assume no liability for the material available on those Internet sites or on other Web sites they may link to. Any comments or suggestions can be sent by e-mail to comments@enslow.com or to the address on the back cover.

♻ Enslow Publishers, Inc., is committed to printing our books on recycled paper. The paper in every book contains 10% to 30% post-consumer waste (PCW). The cover board on the outside of each book contains 100% PCW. Our goal is to do our part to help young people and the environment too!

Illustration Credits: Art Resource, NY, p. 9; Associated Press, pp. 46, 108; Enslow Publishers, Inc., p. 75; The Granger Collection, New York, pp. 1, 4, 11, 17, 28, 91; Library of Congress, pp. 7, 14, 23, 26, 28, 31, 37, 38, 54, 69, 85, 94; Minnesota Historical Society, pp. 73, 78; National Archives and Records Administration, p. 87; Printroom.com Photography, p. 25, 34, 51, 53, 66, 97, 100, 105; State Historical Society of Missouri, pp. 13, 21, 40, 42, 50, 60, 63, 70, 83; Time & Life Pictures/Getty Images, p. 96; © Warner Bros. / Courtesy Everett Collection, p. 107.

Cover Illustration: Printroom.com Photography (Portrait of Jesse James).

CONTENTS

Jesse James

"The Most Daring Robbery on Record"

F ewer than twenty people lived in the southeastern Missouri village of Gads Hill. There were three houses there and one small store. The village was surrounded by pine trees and nestled in the Ozark Mountains. Gads Hill was remote and quiet, just like the serene country home of British author Charles Dickens it was named after. By all accounts, Gads Hill was an unexciting place. That is until Jesse James and his gang arrived on January 31, 1874.

Gads Hill's tranquility and remote, forested location perfectly fit into James's plans. That is why he was there. When he and four other masked men trotted their horses to the general store in the middle of that Saturday afternoon, the quiet village was no longer peaceful. First, the gang robbed the store, taking the owner's gun and eight hundred dollars.[1]

It was a decent amount of money, but the bandits had their eyes on a bigger prize. To get it, they would need to get to the tracks of the Iron Mountain Railroad.

The bandits took the shopkeeper with them. Then, so no one could escape and warn of what was happening, they rounded up the rest of the villagers and escorted them there, too. Next to the tracks, they built a large bonfire to protect everyone from the cold winter weather. The Little Rock Express was due to arrive shortly from St. Louis, about one hundred miles to the north. The train was the gang's big prize.

When the small train finally came into view, a member of James's gang stood on the track, waving a red flag. The conductor knew precisely what that meant. It meant there was danger ahead. But he and his twenty-five passengers had no idea how bad that danger was going to be. In case the train did not stop, James and the other bandits had flipped a switch that would make it leave the main line onto the sidetrack.

It turned out the red flag was all that was needed. When the conductor saw it, he immediately slowed the train and hopped off to see what was going on. That turned out to be a bad move. One of the masked bandits grabbed the conductor and told him, "Stand still, or I'll blow the top of your . . . head off."[2] The bandit then yelled at those inside the train: "If a shot is fired out of the car, I will kill the conductor."[3]

The other gunmen emerged from their hiding places and boarded the train. Some went into the baggage car. They opened the safe, and ripped open the mail. Two of the bandits went into the passenger cars. They announced their intentions to the frightened riders. They were not going to rob ladies or "workingmen."[4] The bandits demanded that all the men show them the palms of their hands. If their hands had calluses, the men were not robbed. The bandits believed those were the workingmen. Those men generally did not have a lot of money, and what they did have they labored hard for. If the men's hands were smooth, it likely meant they were the wealthier Northern businessmen, such as bankers, doctors, and lawyers. They were the ones who were robbed, although the bandits did rob one woman of four hundred dollars.[5]

Jesse James's gang said they only wanted to rob the Northern businessmen during the Gads Hill train robbery. This is a poster from an early silent movie, The Great Train Robbery, *about a band of outlaws, like Jesse James.*

Money was not the only motive for James and his gang. They also were looking for anyone associated with a man named Allan Pinkerton. Pinkerton owned a detective agency that had been hunting James and his gang for some time. Now, the roles were reversed. The gang was looking for him. They had been told he might be on the train. They tore the train apart looking but did not find Pinkerton or any of his agents.

When they finished looting the passengers, the bandits bid the conductor farewell. Before leaving, one of the gang members handed a note to a passenger. It had been written before the robbery. The bandits demanded it be sent to a newspaper in St. Louis. The note was titled, "The Most Daring Robbery on Record."[6] It said the train was stopped by "five heavily armed men and robbed of _____ dollars."[7] The robbers left the amount of money blank for someone else to fill in. When the note was written, the bandits had no idea how much money the train would have on board.

They had escaped on horseback into the dense forest. They would return to rob another day.

Even after the robbery, no one knew exactly what dollar amount should have been written in the blank. Estimates range from two thousand to twenty-two thousand dollars.[8] Whatever the amount, the bandits' message ran in several newspapers. With it was the complete story of the first peacetime train robbery in Missouri history. Of course, by then the bandits were long gone. They had escaped on horseback into the dense forest. They would return to rob another day.

Jesse James and his gang committed the first peacetime train robbery in Missouri history. This lithograph by Thomas Hart Benton entitled Jesse James *shows the James gang robbing a train at gunpoint.*

James and his gang had been robbing for years. Oftentimes, James felt newspapers got their facts wrong when reporting his crimes. He sent the note because he wanted to make sure everything was accurate this time. He was creating his own legend. The Gads Hill robbery helped continue the myth that James was like the celebrated character Robin Hood, who was said to have robbed from the rich to give to the poor. Robin Hood fought for justice. Many believed that is what James did. They believed he only robbed from the rich, as he had at Gads Hill. It was a simple legend James spent much of his life trying to create. The true story of the notorious outlaw's life is much more complicated and a lot less flattering.

2

War at the Border and Beyond

Georgetown College was just ten years old when Robert Sallee James arrived there in 1839. The son of a minister, James had an interest in studying religion, and the Baptist school provided the perfect place for him to do so. The college in Georgetown, Kentucky, was two hundred miles from his home, but the twenty-one-year-old James was more than excited to be there.

James earned a degree during his time in Kentucky, and he also met his wife there. Zerelda Cole, a student at a Catholic school for girls in nearby Lexington, met James at a revival meeting.[1] The two quickly fell in love, and married in December 1841. The bride was only sixteen years old. She was so young that she had to get a relative's approval to wed.

A Home in Clay County

Zerelda's mother lived in Clay County, Missouri, and the newlyweds traveled there in 1842. The area reminded them of Kentucky, which they both loved, and they decided to make it their home. They built a small cabin on some farmland near the tiny town of Centreville. The town, today known as Kearney, was about thirty miles northeast of the much-larger city of Kansas City.

Robert James farmed his land and also became pastor of the New Hope Baptist Church. In little time, he became one of the area's most important citizens. He helped create churches and played a role in the founding of William Jewell College in Liberty, Missouri.[2] In 1843, the couple's first son, Alexander Franklin James, was born. His family called him Frank. Two years later, Zerelda James gave birth to a second son, Robert Jr. He died about a month after he was born. Despite the tragedy, the James family continued to grow. On September 5, 1847, Zerelda gave birth to a son, Jesse Woodson James. In 1849, the couple's only daughter, Susan Lavenia James was born.

The James family owned seven slaves who helped with work on the farm and chores around the home.[3] Life seemed settled for the James family, and farming went well. But Robert James had bigger plans. When a group of men from Missouri left to seek gold in California, he decided to temporarily leave his wife, his three young children, and his church to join them. Some believe he wanted to preach to the gold seekers.[4] Others believe he wanted to search for gold.[5] Either way, the father's departure was not easy

Jesse's father, Robert Sallee James, was a farmer and a pastor in Missouri.

on his young children. One story says three-year-old Jesse held his father, cried, and said, "Don't go, Pa; please don't go away and leave us!"[6]

The California gold rush was well under way by the time Robert James headed west in 1850. Gold seekers from across the country already had traveled to the western state. Everyone wanted a share of the gold that had been discovered there. Some men found it, and they became incredibly wealthy. James hoped he would, too. But he did miss his family and often sent letters home to them. In one letter, he said to "kiss Jesse for me and tell Franklin to be a good boy and learn fast."[7] But James did not find the riches he sought in California. Instead, he became sick. Shortly after he arrived in California, James

Gold miners in California. Robert James went to California during the gold rush in 1850. Like many men who went there, he died in search of gold.

died of cholera, an intestinal infection, at age thirty-two. Years later, Frank and Jesse James visited the city where their father had been buried. They tried to find his grave but could not.[8] The grave was unmarked.

The widowed Zerelda James married twice after her husband died. First, she married Benjamin Simms, a farmer. The marriage did not last long. The bride was much younger than her new husband, and Simms treated her children poorly. On at least one occasion, he whipped Frank.[9] Divorces were not as common in the 1800s as they are today, but historians believe Zerelda considered one. But it never came to that. Simms died a little more than a year after the marriage. The following

California Gold Rush

On January 24, 1848, James Marshall found a small nugget of gold at the site of Sutter's Mill, where he worked in California's Sacramento Valley. Marshall knew his discovery was an important one. But he had no idea how it would impact and reshape the entire United States.

When word of his discovery spread, people from across the United States made their way to California. Men of all professions abandoned their families in search of fortune in California. People from other countries, such as China and Chile, came to California, too. Much of the world, it seemed, had "gold fever." During the next six years, hundreds of thousands of people came to California. Some became extremely wealthy. But most did not find what they were looking for. Some never even made it to their destination and died on the way there. Others died when they got there, from diseases, accidents, and acts of violence. Those who returned home often left California empty-handed. Even James Marshall did not make any money off gold—and he was the one who had discovered it. But the face of California, which was not even a state when the gold rush began, changed forever. So did the lives of many others that traveled there.

year, 1855, the two-time widow married a doctor named Reuben Samuel. He was three years younger than his new wife, and he treated her children better than Simms had. He even became their legal guardian. He and Zerelda eventually had four children: Sallie, John, Fannie, and Archie.

Childhood in Missouri

Jesse had just turned eight years old when his mother married for the third time. Not much is known about his childhood. And his life has been written about so many times, it is often hard to separate fact from fiction. One author wrote that young Frank and Jesse enjoyed torturing animals. He said they would cut off the ears and tails of dogs and cats and remove the wings of birds.[10] However, most historians believe this to be false. They believe Frank and Jesse were typical farm boys who helped with chores, sang songs in church, and frequently studied the Bible. The condition of Jesse's Bible seemed to support that story. His pastor said, "Never in my life had I seen a Bible so marked up, showing such constant usage."[11]

Life on the rural James farm should have been peaceful. But during the 1850s, life was rarely calm anywhere in Clay County, Missouri. The issue of slavery had turned the region around the Missouri-Kansas border into a mini-war zone. The United States was strongly divided on the subject of slavery. The Northern states—such as New Jersey, New York, and Massachusetts—were considered "free" states. The free states did

Jesse James lost his father at a young age.

not allow slavery. The Southern states—such as Georgia, Texas, and Virginia—were slave states. They wanted to stay that way. Missouri, a Southern state, allowed slavery. Kansas had not yet become a state, but the territory—and a majority of its people—were against slavery. This made for some intense fighting between the residents of Missouri and Kansas.

In 1854, Congress passed the Kansas-Nebraska Act. The law called for popular sovereignty in those two territories. People in Missouri and Kansas—and all other new territories—were free to choose whether they wanted to allow slavery within their borders. The people of Missouri wanted Kansas to choose to become a slave state. Bitter battles were fought over this issue. Neighbors with different beliefs even fought one another. Kansans would invade Missouri and capture slaves, carrying them to freedom.[12] People from Missouri would invade Kansas and vote proslavery in the territory's elections.[13] There are many examples of fighting. In one fight that happened in 1858, a Kansan named John Brown led a raid into Missouri and freed eleven slaves and killed a slaveowner.[14] Antislavery guerrillas from Kansas were called jayhawkers. Proslavery guerrillas from Missouri were called bushwhackers. That is because they would hide among the forests and bushes so they would not be caught before or after they had attacked.

Growing up in this environment had a big impact on everyone living in the area. Children believed violence was a way of life. That environment certainly affected the lives of Frank and Jesse James. And the

Roots of Slavery

Slavery is a system in which some people are owned by others and are made to do work for them. Slaves did not have freedom. Slavery had been a part of U.S. culture for more than two hundred years by the time Jesse James was born. It has been traced back as far as 1619. That year, a group of Africans was brought to the colony of Jamestown, Virginia. They were immediately put to work on tobacco farms. As the United States grew, more and more black slaves were brought against their will from Africa to help with farming and other tasks. In 1807, the U.S. government voted not to allow slaves to be brought in from outside the country. The law became effective in 1808. But those who already were in the United States remained enslaved and could be traded from state to state.

violence would get much worse and become far more widespread.

The Civil War Begins

As Frank and Jesse grew, so did the tensions between the proslavery South and the antislavery North. Southern slave states, including Missouri, seceded, or left, the United States of America, also called the Union. The Southern states formed their own nation, the Confederate States of America. Jefferson Davis became president of the Confederacy. Abraham Lincoln was the president of the Union.

War between the Union and the Confederacy officially broke out on April 12, 1861, when the Confederates attacked Fort Sumter, South Carolina. One month later, eighteen-year-old Frank James joined the fight. His family owned slaves and his state had seceded, so he chose to fight for the Confederacy. Frank James did not look much like a soldier when he left the farm for battle. In fact, he did not even have a uniform.[15] Still, he fought as hard as any soldier could, for a year, at least. In 1862, James was back home on the family farm. He had come down with the measles and was captured by Union troops. They took him prisoner but said they would let him go if he promised not to fight again.[16] While he recovered from his illness, James followed the orders. When he regained his health, he broke them. In 1863, a merciless man named William Clarke Quantrill led James back to battle.

Frank James joined the Confederate army in 1861, shortly after the Civil War broke out. This photo of him was taken around 1863.

Quantrill, a former Kansas schoolteacher, led a group of guerrilla fighters. He fought extremely hard for the Confederate cause. Still, many believe he did not believe in the cause and was fighting only for selfish reasons. By 1863, he had built a brutal reputation. He had grown from a common thief who kidnapped slaves and resold them into a cold-blooded killer. He shot many Union soldiers and civilians without remorse.[17] Eventually, Quantrill became known as "the bloodiest man in America."[18]

Frank James met Quantrill in early 1863. He described Quantrill as being "nearly six feet in height, rather thin, his hair and moustache were sandy and he was full of life and a jolly fellow."[19] Quantrill's charming personality and harmless looks had helped lure James into his group, as they did to many young men.

The Youngers

Frank James was not the only recruit Quantrill gathered from the area. The Younger brothers—Cole, Jim, John, and Bob—lived near the James farm. The area's violence had not missed them. All their lives, the brothers had suffered greatly. Union troops had killed their father, Henry Younger, near Kansas City in 1862.[20] Two years earlier, the oldest Younger brother, Dick, had suddenly died. The deaths of those two men tore the Younger family apart.

Cole Younger became the oldest male in the household. He had planned to attend the same college his older brother had but changed his mind. If he had

The Civil War had a tragic impact on the Younger family. This group photo of the Younger family taken many years after the war shows Bob (left), Henrietta (top), Cole (right), and Jim (bottom).

gone to college, his life would have been dramatically different. Instead, the eighteen-year-old wanted to fight for the Confederacy. So he, along with twenty-year-old Frank James, rode off as members of Quantrill's Raiders. They killed those they called their enemies. They robbed stores. Occasionally, they ended up back on the James family farm. They were always welcome there. Zerelda Samuel, as could be expected, supported the raiders' cause. Fifteen-year-old Jesse also supported his brother's new gang. He wanted to join them, but the fighters would not allow him to because he was too young. So he helped them however he could. One way was by loading the bandits' guns. It was not as dangerous as fighting, but it still was a risky task. Legend has it that Jesse blew off the tip of his left middle finger while loading a gun for Quantrill's group.[21] Instead of cursing from the pain, Jesse shouted out "Dingus!" The word became Jesse's nickname and stuck with him for the rest of his life.[22]

The connection Quantrill's Raiders had with the James farm placed the entire family in danger. This became evident shortly after Frank James joined the group. In May 1863, a group of Union soldiers invaded the farm. They were looking for Quantrill's Raiders, and the farm was one place where the group was known to hang out. The guerrillas were not there, but young Jesse was. The soldiers grabbed the teenager around the throat. They beat him up. Then they surrounded his stepfather, Dr. Samuel. They wanted to know where the guerrillas were. But Samuel refused to give them any information. So the soldiers tied a rope around his neck and tossed it over a tree. They hanged him there to make him talk.[23]

Zerelda watched it all happen and screamed in horror. Gasping for air and clinging to life, her husband finally gave in. One of the militiamen said later, "He led the boys into the woods a short distance, and there . . . was discovered the whole band."[24]

Gunshots tore through the brush. Some members of Quantrill's gang were shot and killed.[25] The rest scrambled off with the soldiers in pursuit. Frank James and the rest of the guerrillas escaped by either swimming with their horses or using a quickly built raft to cross the Missouri River.[26]

William Clarke Quantrill, known as "the bloodiest man in America," led a group of guerrilla fighters during the Civil War.

The nearly catastrophic event changed life on the James farm. Samuel went to jail for helping support Quantrill's gang. Zerelda Samuel soon went to jail, too. Jesse's parents and older brother were gone. Only fifteen, Jesse was left in charge of the tobacco fields, the slaves, and his younger sister. The devastation caused by the Union troops made him want to join the Confederacy's fight even more. Jesse wanted revenge.

3

Raiders on the Rampage

Jesse James remained in charge of his family's farm for about one week until his mom was released from jail. By all indications, the time alone—and the frightening raid on his family's farm—had changed Jesse. His hate for the Union grew stronger. He wanted to join his brother in battle. That was if his brother had survived the Union's attack. For a long time, no one knew if Frank James had escaped or had been killed. It soon became clear he had survived when his name was mentioned in a newspaper article in August about an attack on a man near Liberty, Missouri. Quantrill's Raiders were stronger than ever and were about to do more damage than they ever had. Lawrence, Kansas, was where it would occur.

Attack on Lawrence

Everyone knew the eastern Kansas city was the home of many leaders of the antislavery movement. So, destroying Lawrence would make a big statement for Quantrill's Raiders. The raiders knew this and spent a long time planning to do just that. They chose August 21, 1863, as the day to carry out their plan. Shortly after five A.M. on Friday, Quantrill, Frank James, and about 450 other fighters stormed into Lawrence. The town's two thousand residents, most still sleeping, were caught completely by surprise. They had no defense planned and were overwhelmed.

As the raiders rode their horses down Main Street, they shot every man in sight. They looted stores and burned many houses to the ground. In one case, a group of guerrillas broke into a home and asked for the man of the house. When he came downstairs, "they shot [him] in the presence of his young wife and three children."[1] They then made their way through the home, taking all valuables they could find. Before they left, they set the home on fire. The raiders would not even let the man's wife take her husband's body from the home.[2]

A group of the raiders eventually gathered at the Eldridge House. The four-story hotel was the largest

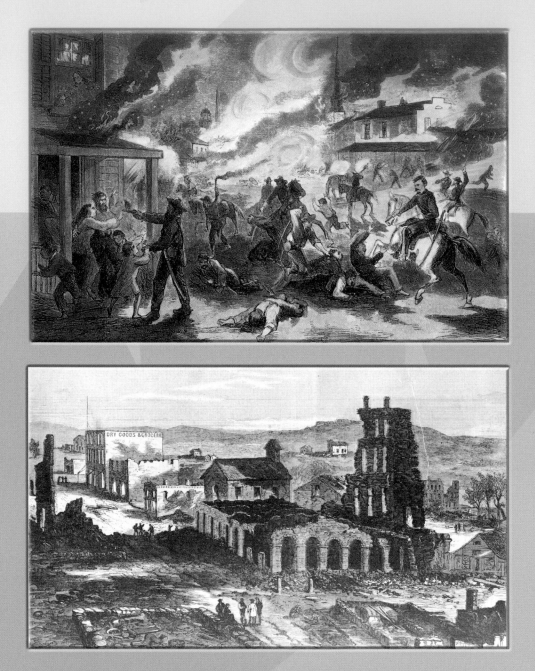

William Clarke Quantrill led his Confederate guerrillas to Lawrence, Kansas, on August 21, 1863. They destroyed the town and killed many of its inhabitants (top). The print below shows the ruins of Lawrence after the attack.

building in town and the finest hotel west of the Mississippi River. Most of the hotel's guests still slept when the raiders arrived outside. The raiders expected people inside to shoot at them from the windows, but no one did. One guest waved a white bedsheet from a window as a sign of surrender. The raiders had captured the hotel guests without a fight.[3] Quantrill led a group of men inside. They robbed the guests and the hotel's safe. All the people were taken out of the building, and then it was set on fire. All that remained of the once-grand hotel, like much of the city's buildings, was a hollow shell.

Outside, the rest of the raiders continued robbing, killing, and pillaging. In the end, they killed more than 150 people and wounded more than twenty.[4] In less than four hours, the once-peaceful town had been left in ruins. Then, the bandits left town as quickly as they had entered it.

> In less than four hours, the once-peaceful town had been left in ruins.

A Brutal Plan

Retaliation against the raiders came, but it was not very efficient. A hastily put together posse, including some Union forces, chased the group as it fled. Several raiders were killed. But most scattered and escaped into the Missouri brush country. Within a few days, the Union forces had a plan to get them out.

On August 25, 1863, Brigadier General Thomas Ewing Jr. of the Union army enacted a bold and brutal

The Eldridge Hotel

The Eldridge House in Lawrence, Kansas, had its share of troubles before and after Quantrill's Raiders burned it to the ground in 1863. The hotel was built by settlers in 1855 and named the Free State Hotel. The name was symbolic. The settlers wanted to let people know that Kansas should be a "free" state, and not support slavery.[5] But only a year later, proslavery Sheriff Sam Jones and a group of men torched the hotel and left it in ruins. The hotel was quickly rebuilt by Colonel Shalor Eldridge. After Quantrill's gang destroyed it, the hotel was rebuilt again and given a new name: The Eldridge Hotel. Soon, the years began to take their toll on the building. By 1925, the hotel was so rundown it had to be torn down and rebuilt. Business improved for a while, but in 1970, the hotel was turned into apartments. In 1985, it was renovated and turned back into a hotel. Twenty years later, the hotel was again renovated. Today, it features a bar named The Jayhawker. Some believe the hotel is haunted. Guests have reported doors opening and shutting by themselves, lights turning off and on, and encounters with ghosts.[6]

plan. It was called General Orders No. 11. The order required all residents of a few western Missouri border counties to leave their homes. They had fifteen days to do so.[7] No one told them where to go. They just had to leave. The goal was to get rid of all the people who were taking care of the guerrilla fighters and to flush out the remaining fighters. With winter on its way, thousands of families evacuated their homes. All the property and possessions they could not carry with them were destroyed. Crops and livestock in the area were destroyed. All buildings were to be burned to the ground.[8]

Thomas Ewing Jr. enacted a brutal plan in retaliation against Quantrill's Raiders.

The many fleeing refugees suffered greatly. One person said there were masses of "poor people, widows and children, who, with little bundles of clothing, are crossing the river to be subsisted by the charities of the people . . . [t]ender and gentle women . . . driving oxen and riding upon miserable broken-down horses without saddles."[9]

Many believed the order to be a form of cruelty. They called it "inhuman, unmanly and barbarous."[10] Others believed it was fair. After all, many of these citizens were aiding the guerrillas. And the guerrillas were breaking the law, killing, and robbing.

More Battles

Quantrill and his band of hundreds of men left Missouri and headed south. On October 6, the guerrillas fought Union forces in southeast Kansas. Many of the guerrillas were disguised as Union army soldiers. They attacked Major General James G. Blunt and his troops. Quantrill's men killed eighty federal soldiers and wounded many more in the bloody battle. One report said dead bodies were "scattered and strewn over the ground for over a mile or two. . . . "[11] Twenty or so of those bodies were Quantrill's men.[12] Luckily for Quantrill, his best-known fighters were not killed. Among the survivors were Frank James, Cole Younger, and William T. "Bloody Bill" Anderson.

The surviving raiders fled to Texas for the winter. At first, the Confederate soldiers there welcomed them as heroes. But the actions of the outlaws while they were in Texas soon changed people's opinions. The raiders robbed farmers. They stole from stores. And they were doing this in a state that was supposed to be on their side. One local Confederate leader said of Quantrill: "[C]ertainly we cannot, as a Christian people, sanction a savage, inhuman warfare, in which men are to be shot down like dogs, after throwing down their arms and holding up their hands supplicating for mercy."[13] Even during a time of war, there are certain rules that are supposed to be followed. But Quantrill's Raiders did not follow rules. They did as they pleased.

In Texas, Quantrill's group split apart. Some members formed their own outlaw groups. In April 1864, Frank James's group returned to Clay County, Missouri. The men he brought with him to the family farm were among the most vicious fighters around. Again, young Jesse James watched and learned from the guerrillas. Shortly, he became one of them.

Becoming a Guerrilla Fighter

Sixteen-year-old Jesse did not look like a fighter. The only known photograph of him from the time shows a baby-faced recruit in a guerrilla uniform that is far too big for him. He is holding a gun in his right hand and has two others in his belt. Historians guess he was about five-and-a-half-feet tall and weighed somewhere around 115 pounds. He may not have looked the part of a bandit, but he certainly played it well.

"Bloody Bill" Anderson was Jesse's first leader. As had Cole Younger's dad, Anderson's father had been killed by those who favored the Union. He had revenge on his mind, too. He was ruthless in his search for it.

Jesse helped Anderson achieve his goal. He quickly became one of Anderson's best men. Anderson said Jesse was "the keenest and cleanest fighter in the command."[14] Jesse was good with guns and horses, and Anderson led him into several battles. In one of his first fights, Jesse was shot in the chest. He was not expected to survive but recovered quickly.[15]

Jesse James became a guerrilla fighter in 1864. This portrait taken around 1864 shows him wearing his guerrilla uniform and holding a gun.

On September 27, 1864, Jesse James, Anderson, and eighty other men attacked the small railroad town of Centralia, Missouri. The bandits stormed through the town, robbing and burning stores. When a stagecoach rolled through, they robbed its passengers. The whistle of an incoming passenger train stopped the robbery.

He may not have looked the part of a bandit, but he certainly played it well.

The express train's crew spotted the guerrillas and decided to blow through town without stopping. But the bandits had blocked the tracks, and the train was forced to stop. The day got more vicious from there. Jesse James and the other guerrillas robbed 125 passengers of their possessions. The twenty-five unarmed Union soldiers on board suffered a far worse fate. The guerrillas stripped the soldiers of their uniforms and gunned them down. Someone who later came across the dead bodies said, "Most of them were beaten over the head, seventeen of them were scalped. . . . Every man was shot in the head. One man had his nose cut off."[16] The goal of this brutality was to scare their enemies off with sheer terror. The guerrillas also set fire to the train depot and the train. Union sergeant Tom Goodman was the only one allowed to live. He was taken hostage but eventually escaped. He later wrote a book about the incident.[17]

The destruction did not end at the train tracks. Major A. V. E. Johnston of the Union army led a force to find the guerrillas. On horseback, the guerrillas attacked the soldiers, and killed more than one hundred of them. Frank James later said his brother Jesse was the one who shot and killed Major Johnston.[18] That never has been confirmed.

However, Union forces did kill many of the guerrillas. In October 1864, "Bloody Bill" Anderson was killed during an ambush. To show off, troops took photos of Anderson's dead body. Then they cut off his head, put it on top of a telegraph pole, and dragged his headless body through the streets.[19] It was common practice for fighters to keep body parts from their victims as souvenirs to show off what they had done and who they had killed.

Confederacy Loses the War

The pro-Confederate guerrillas were suffering some major losses. The Confederate army was, too. The ultimate loss came on April 9, 1865, when General Robert E. Lee of the Confederate army surrendered to Union forces led by General Ulysses S. Grant. The Civil War officially ended later that month. In the meantime, many Confederate supporters continued to fight. On April 14, a Confederate supporter named John Wilkes Booth killed President Abraham Lincoln. Lincoln had signed the Emancipation Proclamation two years earlier, which freed most of the country's slaves.

Many Confederates, including the James brothers, acted as if the war had never ended. But a May 10 battle near Bloomfield, Kentucky, afforded them another big setback. When Quantrill tried to flee from the fight, he was shot in the back.[20] The shooting paralyzed Quantrill from the waist down. He was left in a field but eventually

Confederate General Robert E. Lee (right) surrendered to Union General Ulysses S. Grant on April 9, 1865, at Appomattox Court House in Virginia.

was taken to a military hospital in Louisville, Kentucky. He died in June at the age of twenty-seven.

After Quantrill was shot, Frank James and other bushwhackers surrendered to authorities. After Frank James was granted parole from a general, he headed back home to Missouri. Jesse James also headed home. But his path home was not as smooth as his brother's. On May 15, Jesse was shot in the chest while riding his horse. He later said he tried to surrender but was

The Murder of President Lincoln

On April 14, 1865, President Abraham Lincoln was spending a low-key evening with his wife at Ford's Theatre in Washington, D.C. *Our American Cousin* was the evening's play, and the Lincolns enjoyed the comedy from a balcony. The president had no idea that John Wilkes Booth, an actor and a Confederate supporter, had written his own script for the evening. Shortly after the play began, Booth walked into the balcony where Lincoln was seated and shot the president in the head. He then jumped down to the stage and hurried out of the theater. A doctor ran to Lincoln's side. The president was taken across the street from the theater to a boardinghouse where he was treated. It was no use; Lincoln died the next morning. He was the first president in the history of the United States to be assassinated. Meanwhile, soldiers pursued Booth. On April 26, they caught up with him in Virginia. When he refused to surrender, Booth was shot and killed.

John Wilkes Booth assassinated Abraham Lincoln during a performance of the play Our American Cousin *at Ford's Theatre.*

shot anyway.[21] Another story says Jesse was riding into town with federal marshals, and shot when he tried to escape.[22] It looked like the wound would kill the young rebel, but it did not. Jesse later told a journalist, "On the 15th of May, 1865, I was wounded near Lexington, Mo., in a fight with some Wisconsin cavalry men— soldiers, I believe, of the Second Wisconsin. On the 21st of the same month I surrendered at Lexington. I was in a dreadful fix. A [rifle bullet] had gone through my right lung and everybody thought the wound would be mortal."[23] The bullet stayed in Jesse's body for the rest of his life.[24]

Becoming Bandits

It took months of rest for Jesse James to regain his health after he was shot. A black-and-white photograph taken at the time shows James looking very thin and unhealthy. During the winter of 1866–1867, James said that he "came almost to death's door. My wound would not heal, and I had had several hemorrhages."[1]

Just nineteen years old, James already had been shot twice. His side had lost the Civil War. Soldiers had killed his longtime leader, William Clarke

Quantrill. There were many reasons James should have given up his life of fighting for the quiet of the family farm. But James was not one who often cared about reason. Neither did several other ex-Confederates, including the Younger brothers. Many of them banded together and began a new kind of fight against the Union. They started to rob banks, many of which were owned by Northerners.

The First String of Robberies

One such robbery happened February 13, 1866, in Liberty, Missouri. On that day, a small gang of bandits rode into town in the middle of the afternoon. They stopped in front of the Clay County Savings Bank. Two bandits, dressed in blue Union army outfits, entered Clay County Savings Bank and pointed their pistols at the tellers. The robbers forced the tellers into the bank's vault to fill a sack with money. One of the tellers later said, "He told me that if I did not go in instantly he would shoot me down. I went in."[2] The bandits shut the vault's door with the tellers inside. The bandits made off with nearly sixty thousand dollars.[3]

Few, if any, people outside the bank noticed the robbery taking place. That is, until the tellers discovered the vault's door was not locked and screamed out the bank's window. George Wymore heard the screams and started yelling, too. His shouts were cut short when the bandits shot him dead. Wymore was a student at nearby William Jewell College. It was the same school that Robert James had helped found years earlier. It is

*At age nineteen, Jesse James had
already been shot twice.*

unclear whether Robert's sons, Frank and Jesse, had
anything to do with the robbery. The common belief is
that Frank James and Cole Younger were there, in part
because the men who entered the bank were described
as tall men, which both of them were.[4] Jesse James often
has been placed at the scene, but most historians believe
he was still recovering from his last gunshot wound.
James himself told a journalist that in the spring of
1866 he was "just able barely to mount a horse and ride

about a little."[5] He later said the wound still bothered him in June.[6] If what he said was true, it is doubtful he could have participated in the groundbreaking heist. It was the first successful daytime bank robbery in U.S. history.

Authorities immediately offered a reward for the robbers. The governor of Missouri even formed a militia to help break up the "lawless bands."[7] But the bandits escaped and the bank robberies kept occurring. The next one happened on October 30. Two men entered the Alexander Mitchell and Company bank in Lexington, Missouri, and asked for change for a fifty-dollar bill. They got that and more, leaving with more than two thousand dollars, after robbing the bank at gunpoint. Over the years, historians have linked both Jesse and Frank James to the robbery. If Jesse James was involved, it likely would have been his first bank robbery. But no one ever determined who the robbers were.

Not much is known about the personal lives of Frank and Jesse James during this period. One man who knew Jesse James said he seemed to have settled down after the last time he had been shot. The man said James joined the Baptist church[8] and "was quiet, affable, and gentle in his actions. He was liked by every one who knew him."[9] James still had health problems. He said a doctor told him that "my lung is decayed so badly that I was bound to die and the best thing I could do was to go home and die among my people."[10] Always stubborn, James did not take the doctor's advice. He said, "I did not believe I was going to die."[11] The statement already was pretty clear. James may have been

The Drake Constitution

Exactly why the Jameses and the Youngers began robbing and stealing will likely never be known. However, many historians believe the Drake Constitution had something to do with it. The Drake Constitution became Missouri's new constitution when it was adopted by the government on April 18, 1865. The constitution included an Ironclad Oath, which took voting rights away from anyone other than those who supported the Union. Those who had supported the Confederacy, as the Jameses and the Youngers had, were not allowed to vote or hold office. The constitution also banned anyone who had supported the Confederacy from any kind of professional job. That meant the James brothers, the Younger brothers, and many others were not allowed to become doctors, lawyers, preachers, or teachers. It became very difficult for them to legitimately make money in the state. Many men left Missouri because of the Drake Constitution. Others went along with the state's new laws. The Jameses and the Youngers did neither. They found what they thought to be an easier way to make money by robbing those who had it. Within a few years, the harshest parts of the Drake Constitution were revoked. But by then, the James-Younger gang was deep into its life of crime.

shot twice, but he would not give up the life of banditry. In fact, he began to become more deeply involved in it.

The James Brothers Rob Again

On March 20, 1868, the James brothers and three other men rode their horses into Russellville, Kentucky. One of the men went by the name Thomas Colburn or Coleman. Many historians believe it was most likely Cole Younger, whose full name was Thomas Coleman Younger. Whoever he was, the man and two others entered The Bank of Nimrod L. Long and Company around 2:00 P.M. Colburn/Coleman showed Long a fifty-dollar bill and asked if it was real. Long said it was fake.[12] Having distracted the banker, Colburn/Coleman pulled out a gun and pushed it against Long's head. He demanded all of the bank's money. Long refused and ran for the back door. He made it outside and yelled. Residents exchanged gunfire with the bandits. One man was killed in the shootout.[13] The bandits escaped town with as much as twelve thousand dollars.[14] A few days later, authorities tracked down one of the robbers. He was sent to prison for three years.[15] Eight days after the robbery, an article appeared in the *Louisville Daily Journal*. It described four of the robbers in great detail, and it said that detectives were "on the sharp lookout for the scoundrels."[16]

One story at the time was that the bank had been robbed because Jesse James needed the money to move to a warmer place where he could regain his health, possibly even California.[17] Most historians doubt that

James and his gang robbed the Clay County Savings Bank in 1866, making off with nearly sixty thousand dollars. This photo taken March 16, 1982, shows the Clay County Savings Association building.

was true. But more than a year did pass before the James brothers are known to have been involved in another robbery. It was at the Daviess County Savings Association in Gallatin, Missouri, on December 7, 1869. The crime was done differently than some of those committed in the past. This time, the motive appeared to be personal revenge. Jesse James believed the bank teller was Samuel Cox, the man who had killed his former leader, "Bloody Bill" Anderson. James wanted revenge.

After he and Frank entered the bank, Jesse James handed the teller a hundred-dollar banknote and asked for change. When the bank's president, John W. Sheets, began to write out a receipt, Jesse James shot him in the chest and in the forehead. When the bank's clerk ran for the door, Jesse James shot him in the arm. Before he fled, Jesse James grabbed what turned out to be a bundle of worthless papers. The bandits left the bank with only seven hundred dollars. And James did not get revenge, either. It turns out the person he murdered was not the man who had killed Anderson. But it still was a cold-blooded murder.

As he fled the town, Jesse James's horse became spooked and threw him out of the saddle. James crashed to the ground, but his brother rode by and picked him up. The two rode out of town on one horse, leaving James's horse behind. The brothers soon robbed another man of his horse and rode away.

The abandoned horse became a vital clue to people trying to track down the robbers. It was identified as belonging to a "James of Clay County."[18] It was a unique horse and authorities were able to trace it to Jesse James. Two armed men rode south into Liberty and asked the authorities to help them capture the James brothers. Deputy Sheriff John Thompson and his son, Oscar, joined the men. The foursome rode to the James farm.

When they got there, a boy fled the house and ran to the stable. He opened the doors, and out came Frank and Jesse James, riding their horses with their pistols blazing. Shots came from everywhere. The loud explosions spooked the deputy sheriff's horse. It rode off without him and actually caught up with the James brothers with no one aboard. One of the brothers shot and killed the horse.[19] The deputy sheriff took a horse from the farm and the four men rode off after the James brothers. But they were long gone. The authorities offered a hefty three-thousand-dollar reward for their capture.[20] The governor of Missouri added five hundred dollars for each man.[21] They were thieves and killers. He wanted them dead or alive.

Fighting Back With Words

Jesse James fought back against his hunters, this time with words. He told anyone who would listen that he had not been involved in the bank robbery and murder at Gallatin. He said he had sold the horse that had been left at the scene.[22] He also wrote letters to newspapers. In one published in the *Kansas City Times*, James said he was on the run because he was afraid he would be found guilty even though he was not. He wrote that "when I think I can get a fair trial I will surrender to the civil authorities of Missouri. But I will never surrender to be mobbed by a set of blood thirsty poltroons [cowards]."[23] He also wrote he had "lived a peaceable citizen, and obeyed the laws of the United States" since the end of the Civil War.[24]

Some respected citizens provided alibis for Jesse James. Many people believed his claims of innocence. Sympathetic newspaper articles had a lot to do with

The Weapons of Jesse James

Rarely was Jesse James without a gun. But which kind did he use? The answer depends on which point of his life is in question. During the Civil War, Confederate bushwhackers typically used .36 caliber Colt revolvers.[25] These guns could fire six shots without having to be reloaded, which gave their users a big advantage over those who still were using single-shot rifles. The revolvers also were smaller than most guns of the time and easy to hide. The gun had its disadvantages, too. It was not as powerful as a rifle, thus frequently did not kill people with just one shot. The shooter often had to fire another shot to "finish off" his victim. Later in his life of banditry, James began to favor the six-shot Colt Peacemaker, a .45 caliber gun that was more powerful and easier to reload than the .36 caliber Colts he previously had used.[26] This allowed him to carry fewer guns with him on a robbery. James and his fellow bandits also were known to carry shotguns during their robberies.[27]

Journalist John Newman Edwards wrote many articles about Jesse James and helped create the image of James as a heroic bandit.

that fact. Journalist John Newman Edwards wrote a lot of those articles.

The newspapers did not think anyone had much of a chance of catching the James brothers. One story read: "They know every foot-path and by-road . . . they are cool, determined, desperate men, well mounted and well armed."[28] They also knew when to hide.

The Robberies Continue

Frank and Jesse James kept a low profile for a long time after the Gallatin bank robbery. Even James historians do not agree upon where they were. Some believe they traveled from state to state. Others have said they may have been hiding out at home on or near the farm, where they received help from their family and neighbors. Jesse James said he and his brother spent some time in Texas.[1] Many of the crimes that were being committed across the country were being blamed on the brothers.

When they returned from their hiding, the James brothers made sure everyone knew they were back.

Announcing the Robbery

On June 3, 1871, nearly all the residents of Corydon, Iowa, were gathered at the Methodist church. Henry Clay Dean, a popular politician, was giving a speech there. No one wanted to miss it. The bandits knew this and had planned for it. The gathering left the Ocobock Brothers bank nearly wide open. The robbers were believed to be the James brothers, Cole Younger, and Clell Miller. When the four armed bandits arrived at the bank's doorstep, the only person inside was the cashier. The gang forced the man to give them the bank's money. Then they tied him up and took the six thousand dollars they had stolen to the church. They interrupted Dean's speech and announced that the bank had been robbed. Then they left. At first, no one believed them, and Dean continued talking. When people finally realized the bandits were telling the truth, a posse formed to pursue them.

The late-forming band had no luck catching the bandits. So the bank hired Pinkerton's National Detective Agency to try and do so. Pinkerton agents tracked the bandits into Missouri. But they did not catch Frank or Jesse James. Eventually, Clell Miller was caught, arrested, and brought back to Iowa to be tried for the robbery. But thanks to many witnesses who swore he was elsewhere when the bank was robbed, Miller was acquitted.

Jesse and Frank James, along with Cole Younger and Clell Miller, robbed the Ocobock Brothers bank in Corydon, Iowa, on June 3, 1871. This photo of Jesse (left) and Frank James was taken around 1872.

Pinkerton's National Detective Agency

When Pinkerton's National Detective Agency was hired to pursue the James-Younger gang, most thought the gang's days were numbered. Allan Pinkerton, a Scottish immigrant, served as head of the Union Intelligence Service during the Civil War. He allegedly foiled an assassination plot while guarding Abraham Lincoln in 1861 on his way to the president's inauguration. The Union Intelligence Service eventually became the U.S. Secret Service.

Pinkerton had founded his agency in 1850. It was the first-ever detective agency in the United States, and gained a solid reputation as a crime-fighting group. The company's logo featured a picture of a black-and-white eye, underneath which was written the motto, "We Never Sleep." To many criminals, that must have seemed like it was true. Though the company specialized in capturing counterfeiters and train robbers, the agency also took on several other types of cases. All criminals feared Pinkerton and his agents.

Allan Pinkerton, head of Pinkerton's National Detective Agency, chased Jesse James for many years.

Jesse James denied having any role in the Corydon robbery. He wrote a letter to the *Kansas City Times* stating this. The letter read, "As far as Frank and I robbing a bank in Iowa or any where else, it is as base a falsehood as ever was uttered from human lips."[2] He also said, "I can prove, by some of the best citizens in Missouri, my whereabouts on the third day of June, the day the bank was robbed, but it is useless for me to prove an alibi."[3] He thought no one would believe him, but said he would surrender—if only he thought he could get a fair trial.

The James-Younger Gang's Pattern of Robberies

The Corydon robbery was the beginning of a pattern for the James brothers. After they committed a robbery, they would take some time off to hide out and live off what they had stolen. Then they would rob again. It was a pattern likely based on their need for money. Eleven months after the robbery in Corydon, the brothers struck again.

On April 29, 1872, Jesse and Frank James, Cole Younger, and two others rode into the town of Columbia, Kentucky. Two of the men jumped off their horses and went inside the Bank of Columbia. The others stood guard outside. The bank's cashier, R. A. C. Martin, immediately knew what was going on when he saw the men. He refused to open the bank's main vault, and one of the bandits shot him dead. Three other men in the bank escaped unharmed. The bandits rode out of town without being pursued. They made off with six hundred dollars.[4] That small amount of money certainly would not last long, especially when split five ways. So, not surprisingly, the gang did not wait long before its next heist. However, the location they chose to commit the crime was a surprise.

Thousands of people gathered at the Kansas City fair on September 26, 1872. During the middle of the day, Frank and Jesse James, and one other man, rode their horses up to the fair's ticket booth. One of the men—all wearing bandannas over their faces—jumped off his horse and approached the ticket booth. He grabbed the cash box and put all the money in his pocket. When the cashier ran out of his booth and tried to retrieve the cash, a shot was fired that hit a young girl in the leg. The bandits left with $978.[5] If they would have come thirty minutes earlier, they would have had twelve thousand dollars.[6] That is because most of the booth's funds had just been collected and put in a safe place.

> They committed the robbery in the middle of the day, in front of thousands of people.

What the bandits did was clearly wrong. Journalist John Newman Edwards thought so, too. But he also thought the bandits were so daring that their actions should be admired. After all, they committed the robbery in the middle of the day, in front of thousands of people. A large number of police had been working the fairgrounds. But the robbers still made an easy getaway. A former Confederate soldier, Edwards made the James-Younger gang's actions sound exciting and romantic. He wrote that the bandits were "so diabolically daring and so utterly in contempt of fear that we are bound to admire it and revere its perpetrators."[7] He also wrote: "What they did we condemn. But the way they did it we cannot help admiring."[8]

The Wild West's Robin Hood

Edwards's words had a large impact on the way people perceived Frank and Jesse James, as well as the other gang members. He made them sound like folk heroes. To him they were folk heroes, similar to Robin Hood, who legend says robbed from the rich and gave to the poor. In this case, the "rich" were the Northerners and the "poor" were the Southerners. Many people began believing that is what the gang did. The bandits often perpetuated that falsehood. One gang member, most likely Jesse James, wrote a letter to the *Kansas City Times*. It said that they "rob from the rich and give to the poor."[9] To this day, some people still believe that is what James and his gang did.

What they really did, of course, was rob for their own greedy and selfish reasons. They killed innocent people, and stole money from anyone they could. And soon they were back at it again. On May 27, 1873, four men robbed the Ste. Genevieve Savings Association in Ste. Genevieve, Missouri. No one was hurt in the robbery, but about four thousand dollars was stolen.[10] The St. Louis police said members of the James-Younger gang were involved in the robbery.[11] At least one historian believes Frank and Jesse James, and Cole and John Younger committed the robbery.[12] One robbery the James brothers certainly were involved in happened July 21, 1873, in the western Iowa town of Adair. The town was not even a year old—and definitely unprepared for a train robbery—when the bandits struck.

"We Want Money!"

Before the train rolled into town, the men loosened a piece of the Chicago, Rock Island and Pacific Railroad track it would be traveling over. They then tied a rope to the loose piece. When the train came close, they yanked on the rope and the piece of rail came off the track. John Rafferty, the engineer, saw this and tried to stop the train before it got to that point. But it was too late. The engine car flipped onto its side, killing Rafferty. Some passengers were hurt, too. One of them later said the masked bandits boarded the train with their guns raised. He said the bandits' leader said, "Give us those keys . . . or I'll blow your brains out! . . . We want money! Where's them safe keys—quick or some of you will get killed."[13]

> "Where's them safe keys—quick or some of you will get killed."

The bandits raided the coach cars. But what they were really looking for was not there. The safe full of gold they were hoping to find was on a train that was

History of Train Robbing

Though many believe they were the first to rob a train, the James brothers were not the first. On October 6, 1866, a gang headed by brothers John and Simeon Reno robbed a train in Indiana of several thousand dollars. Theirs was the first peacetime train robbery in U.S. history. Coincidentally, Allan Pinkerton's detective agency was involved in that case, too, and helped capture the brothers. But not before the Reno brothers robbed other trains. But when most people think about train robberies, Frank and Jesse James most often are the ones thought of first.

scheduled to pass by the next day. The James-Younger gang had the wrong train and rode off with about two thousand dollars.[14] The railroad offered a large reward for their capture, but the bandits got away. They went back to Missouri. A few months later, Jesse James wrote a letter to a newspaper denying he or his brother had taken part in the robbery. The gang's first train robbery was a moderate success, at least financially. Now it was time for them to attempt another type of robbery for the first time.

THE TRAIN ROBBERY.

Jesse James Says He is Innocent and Presents the Proof.

We clip the following from the Kansas City Times:

Whenever a train robbery or a bank cracking operation transpires in any portion of the United State, the James and Younger boys receive all the censure. They are the first names mentioned, and all the blame, all the criminality, is centered upon them. The majority of the people living in this section of the country do not believe that Jesse and Frank James or the Younger boys are guilty of all the great robberies charged against them during the past few years. But it is so very convenient for unsophisticated Cincinnati and St. Louis detectives, who desire to achieve renown, to make costly and nonsensical campaigns against the James and Youngers, that they brand each and every robbery with the name of these ubiquitous outlaws—and then, after riding roughshod over the farming population of Western Missouri, claim great credit and wagon loads of laurels for a successful campaign.

FOOLISH DETECTIVES.

The James and Younger boys could, and would, have been captured long ago by the native detectives and officials had the proper inducements been offered to indemnify them against loss, and the consequent danger incurred in such a task. But aside from the fact that no positive proof existed that the James or Younger boys were implicated in the robberies charged against them, the authorities that be sought in Chicago, Cincinnati, St. Louis and other Eastern cities, for common "thief-catchers who dare not be seen out in our backwoods at night, and who hunt outlaws on special trains on a railroad, drive all over the country in fancy carriages enquiring of farmers if they have seen the James boys lately, and to make a show of diligence outrage farmhouses, carry off peaceable citizens, kill twelve-year old boys, blow off the arms of old women, and waylay poor, tired reporters

JESSE JAMES PROTESTS.

The fact that Jesse and Frank James had been seen in this city several times during the week previous to the Otterville robbery was common gossip in the city. One of the boys was at Tony Pastor's Concert in this city just before the raid. Jesse James, who occasionally visits his relatives in this city, is now residing in Kansas, a peaceable citizen, under a false name. He reads the daily papers, and keeps posted as to what goes on. Last evening a friend of his rode up to one of the reporters of the Times and handed him the following letter. He was not either Jesse or Frank James, but was much younger than either of them. The letter is as follows:

OAK GROVE, KANSAS, Aug. 14, 1876.

To the Kansas City Times:

You have published Hobbs Kerry's confession which makes it appear that the James and the Youngers were the Rocky Cut robbers. If there was only one side to be told, it would probably be believed by a good many people that Kerry has told the truth. But his so called confession is a well built pack of lies from beginning to end. I never heard of Hobbs Kerry, Charles Pitts, and Wm. Chadwell until Kerry's arrest. I can prove my innocence by eight good and well known men of Jackson County and show conclusively that I was not at the train robbery. But at present I will only give the names of two of those men to whom I refer for proof. Early on the morning after the train robbery east of Sedalia, I saw the Hon. D. S. Gregg, of Jackson county, and talked with him 30 or 40 minutes. I also seen and talked to Mr. Thomas Pitcher, of Jackson county, the morning after the robbery. Those two men's oaths cannot be impeached. So I refer the Grand Jury of Cooper county, Mo., and Gov. Hardin to those men before they act so rashly on the oath of

A LIAR, THIEF AND ROBBER.

Kerry knows that the James and Youngers can't be taken alive, and that is why he has put it on us. I have referred to Messrs. Pitcher and Gregg because they are prominent men, and they know I am innocent and their word can't be disputed. I will write a long article to you for the Times, and send it to you in a few days, showing fully how Hobbs Kerry has lied. Hoping the Times will give me a chance for a fair hearing and vindicate myself through its columns, I will close. Respectfully,

J. W. JAMES.

The above letter is published for what it is worth. It has this recommendation to credence

On January 15, 1874, the gang robbed its first stagecoach near Hot Springs, Arkansas. Hot Springs was a popular place for rich travelers, who came to soak in the area's hot thermal spring waters. For years, people had used the waters as a treatment for many types of illnesses. When the robbers stopped the stagecoach, they asked the passengers if any of them had been a Confederate soldier during the Civil War. One man said he had. The bandits gave him back the money and the watch they had taken from him. The robbers were trying to maintain the reputation that they only stole from Northerners and not Southerners. When Jesse James died years later, a watch from one of the stagecoach's passengers was found among his belongings.[15]

> The robbers were trying to maintain the reputation that they only stole from Northerners and not Southerners.

The bandits quickly returned to robbing trains. They believed that was where they got the big money. Two weeks after the stagecoach robbery, they robbed another train in Gads Hill, Missouri. Jesse James had written about the robbery even before it occurred. When the masked bandits finished robbing the train's passengers, they left James's note with a passenger. They wanted him to give it to the newspaper. The note was titled "The Most Daring Robbery on Record." It read: "The robbers arrived at the station a few minutes before the arrival of the train and arrested the station agent and put him under guard."[16] It described the robbers as "all large men, none of them under six feet tall. They were all masked and started in a southerly direction after they had robbed the express."[17]

The note helped add to the legend of Jesse James and the rest of the outlaws he ran with. So had a lengthy newspaper article written a few months earlier by John Newman Edwards. The story was titled "A Terrible Quintette," and appeared in the *St. Louis Dispatch*. The terrible quintette was Jesse James, Frank James, Cole Younger, John Younger, and Arthur McCoy. Edwards claimed to have interviewed the men for his story. The story gave alibis for each of the bandits for every crime they were accused of. It also told the story of how the James brothers and the Younger brothers had been forced to run from the law since the end of the Civil War. It made them seem like decent guys who had been wronged by society. Many believed Edwards's words were true.

Soon, more newspapers and magazines began writing similar stories about the James brothers. Many of the accounts were exaggerated, but their reputation as men who were fighting for justice grew.

Chapter 6

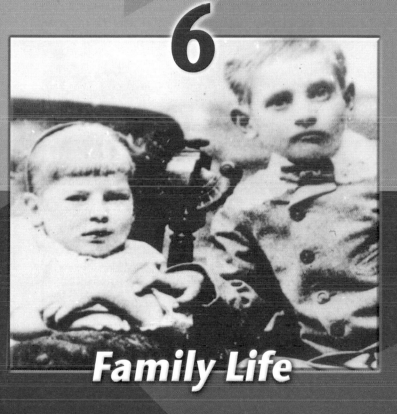

Family Life

gents from Pinkerton's National Detective Agency still were hunting for the James brothers in 1874. It had been two and a half years since the agency had been hired to track the bandits down. On March 10, 1874, it was agent Joseph Whicher's turn. The young man's plan was to get hired to work on the James farm in Clay County. That way, he could get to know Frank and Jesse James and easily capture them.

The last time anyone saw Whicher alive, he was walking toward the farm. The next day, someone found his body. He had been shot in the head and the heart.[1] A few days later, two more Pinkerton detectives were killed in a shootout in Roscoe, Missouri. The two men had crossed paths with two of the Younger brothers, who became suspicious of the agents' motives. One of the agents pulled out a gun and shot John Younger in the neck. Younger returned fire and shot both of the agents. Younger and the two agents died from their wounds.

Marriage to an Outlaw

The governor of Missouri again became involved with trying to capture Jesse James and his group. But the James-Younger gang continued to make everyone look bad. In fact, both Frank and Jesse James lived relatively normal personal lives. Jesse James married his first cousin, Zerelda "Zee" Mimms, on April 23, 1874. She had been his longtime sweetheart and had helped nurse him to health after he had been shot in the lung. At the time of their wedding, the couple had been engaged for nine years. Zee was twenty-eight and Jesse was twenty-six. The Reverend William James married the couple. He was uncle to both the bride and the groom. After the wedding, the newlyweds went to Texas for their honeymoon. It was there that the only photo ever of Jesse James riding a horse was taken.[2] He is seated atop his favorite horse, Stonewall. The horse was named after Confederate general Thomas "Stonewall" Jackson.

John Newman Edwards wrote about James's wedding in the *St. Louis Dispatch*. According to the story, the couple planned to live in Mexico. The article made it sound like the marriage was going to be a good one. It credited the groom as saying, "You can say that both of us married for love, and that there cannot be any sort of doubt about our marriage being a happy one."[3]

Frank James found his own domestic happiness with a schoolteacher named Annie Ralston. Frank and Annie married a couple of months after Jesse and Zee did. Both James brothers started families of their own. They had more than themselves to look after. If they were killed during a shootout, they would leave widows at home. But that did not stop them from their lives of crime.

On December 8, 1874, five members of the James-Younger gang rode into Muncie, Kansas. There was a

Zee James

Zerelda "Zee" James had more in common with her new husband than most new brides do. Not only was she a first cousin of Jesse James, she also had been named after her husband's mother. Following her husband's death, Zee James suffered from depression. She would wear only black clothing, never remarried, and rarely left the house.[4] Until her own death on November 13, 1900, Zee James lived a poor and quiet life.

Jesse James married Zerelda "Zee" Mimms on April 23, 1874.

train station in the small riverside town, and it was about to become the scene of a crime. The bandits forced the train to stop and made a bank worker who was onboard open the safe. The worker said that "one placed a revolver to my head while the other leveled a Henry rifle on the other side, and I was told to unlock the safe."[5]

The train provided the bandits with a gold mine. After the robbery, the gang headed north with some thirty thousand dollars in cash, gold, and goods. Several rewards were offered for the robbers. One of the bandits, Bud McDaniel, was caught a couple of weeks later. He had four guns, some jewelry stolen from the train, and more than one thousand dollars cash in his possession.[6] McDaniel was arrested and questioned, but he never told the names of the other bandits.[7] McDaniel eventually tried to escape and was killed.

The Pinkerton Agency's Embarrassment

The pressure was on officials to capture the rest of the bandits and to stop the robberies. Citizens feared that they might be the next targets of the James-Younger gang. Large amounts of reward money were offered. Pinkerton's National Detective Agency remained on the case but had never made much progress. Jesse James wanted to rub that fact in the agents' faces. He wrote to a newspaper: "Pinkerton has gained great notariety [*sic*] as a Detective, but we have so easily baffled him."[8]

The Pinkerton agency's agents were embarrassed by their lack of success. To remedy this, they attempted a daring move. Late at night on January 26, 1875, the Pinkerton agency made its most risky attempt to capture the James brothers. The agents gathered outside the James farm in Clay County. They surrounded the home, believing Frank and Jesse James were inside. To try and persuade them out, they tossed a fuel-coated firebomb through a window. Dr. Samuel, Jesse James's stepfather, shoveled the bomb into the fireplace before the house caught on fire. Then an explosion went off, hitting Zerelda Samuel in the right arm. Pieces of shrapnel from the explosion also hit eight-year-old Archie Peyton Samuel (James's half-brother) in the stomach. Young Archie died from the hit, and Zerelda had to have part of her right arm amputated.[9] After all this destruction, it turns out Frank and Jesse James were not inside.

The reputation of the Pinkerton agency suffered greatly. People were outraged that they had killed an innocent boy. Newspapers called the attack cowardly. One wrote: "There is no crime, however dastardly, that merits a retribution as savage and fiendish as the one which these men acting under the semblance of law have perpetrated."[10] John Newman Edwards, always a friend to the James brothers, predictably had a strong opinion. He asked for former Confederate soldiers to fight against the Pinkerton agents and even to kill them.[11] He called the Pinkerton agents "dastardly dogs who were hunting human flesh for hire."[12]

The government of Missouri also got involved. A member of the state legislature proposed a bill that would grant complete amnesty to the James brothers, the Younger brothers, and others. If it passed, the gang members could not be punished for all their alleged wrongdoings during the Civil War. It also would make certain they received fair trials for everything they were accused of doing after the war. The measure named Frank and Jesse James and Cole and Jim Younger. It said that "most, if not all of the offenses with which they have been charged have been committed by others, and perhaps by those pretending to hunt them."[13] This was

Allan Pinkerton (center) and two railroad special agents sit for a portrait around 1880. Only five years earlier, Pinkerton's agents attempted to apprehend Jesse James at the James's farm in Missouri. The raid proved to be very unsuccessful.

exactly what Jesse James had said he wanted. If the bill passed, he and the others would be given fair trials. The bill came close to passing and becoming a law, but it did not.

Fatherhood

Zee James was pregnant during the time of the attack on the James farm. On August 31, 1875, she gave birth to a son, Jesse Edwards James. The boy took his first name from his father and his middle name from newspaperman John Newman Edwards. The chosen middle name left little doubt that Edwards and Jesse James were in cahoots. Throughout the years, many would refer to Jesse Edwards as "Jesse Jr."

Jesse Edwards James, "Jesse Jr.," was born on August 31, 1875. This photo shows him (right) with his sister Mary.

The day after Jesse Jr. was born, his father's gang got back to its outlaw ways. One day after Jesse James's twenty-eighth birthday, four bandits robbed a bank in Huntington, West Virginia. They made off with ten thousand dollars.[14] Whether James was involved likely will never be known. Some believe he was. But a description of all four bandits that appeared in a newspaper article does not seem to indicate James's presence. Many believe he was at home with his wife and newborn son in Edgefield, Tennessee. The family had moved to the Nashville suburb shortly before Jesse Jr. was born. Frank and Annie James had moved to Tennessee, too.

Creating an Alias

Moving to Tennessee was not the only way Jesse James attempted to avoid being caught. He also changed his name. His new name was John Davis Howard. His wife's alias was Josie Howard, and Jesse Jr. became Tim Howard. Jesse James's cousin said that the bandit "wanted to quit the business, but he said he had to make a living, and as the whole world seemed to be pitted against him, and he couldn't do anything else, he kept on with it."[15] So he did. Jesse James left Tennessee for long periods. Neighbors said he often would return with large amounts of money. He told them he was a businessman, and a photograph taken at the time shows James looking very much the part. The photo was taken in Nebraska, and it shows James with his hair well groomed. He is wearing a suit and looks nothing like a bandit. Even if his image was always as clean as it was in that photo, the look did not fool everyone. Many of his neighbors remained suspicious of him.

Being away from his usual Missouri haunts did not stop James's robbing. In July 1876, the James and Younger brothers, and a few others returned to central Missouri. Their plan was for another train robbery. On July 6, a Missouri Pacific Railroad train rolled into an area known as Rocky Cut. The bandits were waiting. They already had captured the train's watchman. When the train stopped, the bandits struck. They boarded the train and gathered the keys to its safe. They opened the safe and stole its contents. The bandits fled with around fifteen thousand dollars. They did not rob any passengers.

> Jesse James left Tennessee for long periods. Neighbors said he often would return with large amounts of money.

The robbery made the Pinkertons even more upset. They had failed in every attempt to capture the James brothers. And the bandits still were robbing. The detectives raided several parts of Missouri. A dozen of them even showed up at Frank James's father-in-law's home near Kansas City. They had hoped James would be there. But he was not.[16]

In fact, the James brothers, the Younger brothers, Bill Chadwell, Clell Miller, and Charlie Pitts were hundreds of miles away. They were on their way north to Minnesota. When they got there, they had big plans. But in life, everything does not always go according to plan.

Chapter

7

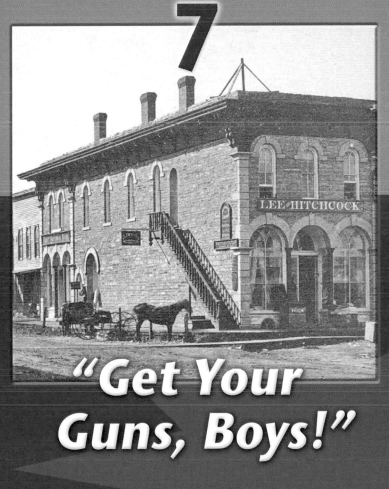

"Get Your Guns, Boys!"

The James-Younger gang toured Minnesota by train when they arrived in August 1876. One of the gang's newest members, Bill Chadwell, had lured them there. He was a Minnesota native, and banks in his home state, he said, would be easy to rob. After considering other sites, they decided on the college town of Northfield. Cole Younger later said, "we went to Northfield in expectation of getting the $75,000 belonging to ex-Governor Ames and General Butler."[1] It was supposed to be easy money.

A Disastrous Robbery

On September 7, the eight-man gang gathered just west of the town. Jesse James, Bob Younger, and Charlie Pitts rode up to the First National Bank. They got off their horses and tied them to posts in front of the bank. As soon as Cole Younger and Clell Miller rode up to the bank, the first three bandits went inside. It appeared as if it was going to be a standard bank robbery. Easy money, just like Chadwell had told them it would be. Then everything went wrong.

It began when a customer tried to enter the bank. Miller grabbed him and the man shouted, "Get your guns, boys! They're robbing the bank!"[2] The townsfolk heard him and were alerted to what was going on inside the bank. Soon, the other three bandits, who had been acting as lookouts a little farther away, joined Miller and Cole Younger. The five men rode through the streets, shooting their guns in the air and telling everyone to stay inside their homes and shops. Most did. One man who remained on the streets, Nicholas Gustavson, was shot in the head. No one knows who shot him; it could have been the bandits or Northfield residents by accident. Gustavson died four days later. Numerous residents fired back at the bandits. Miller was shot and killed by a resident. So was Chadwell. Cole Younger was shot in the hip but survived.

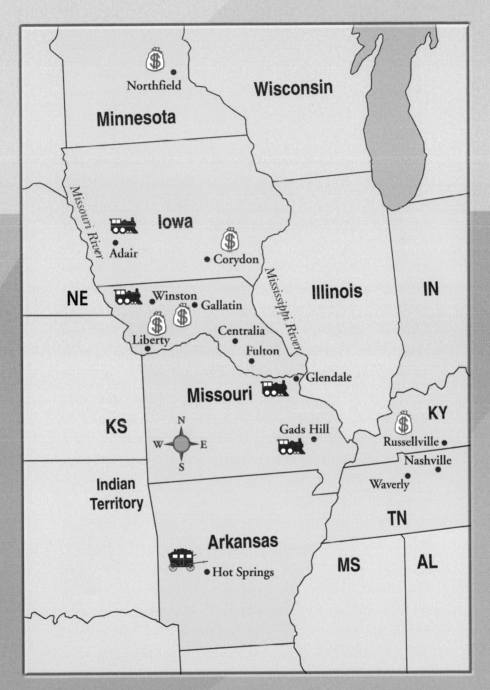

Jesse James committed many robberies across the Midwest. This map shows the towns that fell victim to the James-Younger gang.

There was chaos inside the bank, as well. With their guns drawn, the three bandits inside ordered the cashier, Joseph Lee Heywood, to open the safe. When he refused, one of the bandits cut his throat and smashed a gun against his head. Heywood fell to the floor, victim of another cold-blooded attack. Bank teller Alonzo Bunker made a dash for the door, and Pitts shot him in the shoulder. Bunker survived. The bandits fled the bank themselves, but before they did, one of them fatally shot Heywood in the head. One historian believed it was Jesse James who did that.[3] But all others, including several eyewitnesses, say it was Frank James.[4] On his deathbed, Cole Younger allegedly told two people who Heywood's killer was. But he swore them to secrecy, and they never broke that promise.[5]

As the bandits left the bank, Bob Younger was shot in the elbow. The shot broke his elbow. The six still-living bandits fled the scene through a barrage of gunfire. The entire episode took seven minutes, and the gang left with just $26.70.[6] It was far short of the seventy-five thousand dollars Cole Younger said the gang planned to make off with. It certainly had not been easy money, as Chadwell had said it would be.

This time, there was no trouble-free escape. Hundreds of farmers, townspeople, and law officers joined together to form a large local manhunt. A telegraph was sent to places across the rest of Minnesota. Soon, posses from all over were looking for the gang. One report said: "The number of volunteers was larger than could be armed readily."[7] Many were drawn by the thousands of dollars in reward money that had been

Joseph Lee Heywood

At the time of his death, Joseph Lee Heywood was a popular man in Northfield, Minnesota. He remains beloved there today. There are many tributes to him in town. Carleton College, where Heywood was treasurer, has a Joseph Lee Heywood Society, which recognizes people who have pledged to give future financial support to the school. More than fourteen hundred people are members of the society. The school also is home to a plaque that honors the fallen hero. It reads: "A man modest, true, gentle; diligent in business; conscientious in duty; a citizen benevolent and honorable; towards God reverent and loyal; who, while defending his trust as a bank officer, fearlessly met death at the hands of armed robbers, in Northfield, Sept. 7, 1876."[8]

The Northfield robbery did not go as planned and proved to be the downfall of the James-Younger gang. This photo of Northfield was taken around the time of the robbery.

offered for the bandits' capture. It was the largest manhunt ever in the United States.[9]

The bandits had another disadvantage. The person who had guided them through the rainy and unfamiliar Minnesota territory, Bill Chadwell, was dead. With bloodthirsty people tailing them, the group slowly made its way out of the Northfield area. They stole horses along the way. One of the horses was blind, which slowed the gang down a bit. Sometimes, the men even had to travel on foot. And after a few days, they split into two groups.

Frank and Jesse James went off together. The weary brothers rode west toward the Dakota Territory. Though they were shot at along the way, they kept going. They stole horses several times to help speed their escape. They traveled day and night and made it to the Dakota Territory. From there, they traveled into Iowa. The brothers somehow had managed to shake off all their pursuers. For the most part, they were free—for now.

Capturing the Younger Brothers

The other four members of the James-Younger gang were not as lucky. On September 21, the Younger brothers and Pitts were found near Madelia, Minnesota, some eighty miles west of Northfield. The bandits were trapped in a wooded area with little hope of escaping when a large group of regular citizens finally caught up to them. A gunfight began and ended quickly. Pitts was killed. All three of the Youngers were hit by gunfire and badly wounded. It did not take long for the bandits to surrender. Bob Younger told his hunters, "The boys are all shot to pieces. For God's sake don't kill me."[10] He had been shot in the right side. Cole Younger had been shot in the face. Jim Younger had been shot in the leg and the jaw.[11] Cole Younger had eleven bullet and buckshot wounds and Jim Younger had five.[12]

The wounded Youngers were taken into town by wagon. When they arrived, cheering crowds were all around. The Youngers were taken to jail. They pleaded guilty to their crimes, and were sentenced to life in prison. It was an inglorious end to the powerful and feared James-Younger gang. Over the years, the group had committed twenty-six holdups, killed seventeen men, and stolen more than two hundred thousand dollars.[13] Even today, the residents of Madelia are proud to have played a role in the demise of the feared gang. Each September, the city hosts the Younger Brothers Capture Event. It features a reenactment of the killing of Pitts and the capture of Bob, Cole, and Jim Younger.

The Jameses Keep Quiet

Frank and Jesse James kept low profiles for a long time after the botched Northfield robbery. After all, they were still wanted men, and what had happened in Northfield made them even more so. Both brothers escaped back to their homes in Tennessee. Frank James lived there on a farm just outside Nashville under the assumed name of B. J. Woodson. His wife gave birth to a son, Robert Franklin James, on February 6, 1878. By all accounts, the new father began to live a typical farmer's life. He said, "I worked regularly every day on the farm, seldom failing to put in my full ten hours per day in the field."[14] As much as a wanted criminal could, the oldest James brother began living a normal life.

For a while, Jesse James did, too. The people in Humphreys County, Tennessee, knew him as farmer J. D. Howard. In 1878, Zee James gave birth to twin sons. But the boys died shortly afterward. The next year, the couple's only daughter, Mary Susan James, was born.

As Woodson and Howard, the brothers remained inseparable. One man who knew them at the time said they were "always together. Woodson rarely ever had anything to say, while Howard spoke occasionally, and even then only when a question was asked."[15]

Unlike his older brother, Jesse James was not ready to leave the life of banditry for a simple family life. He raced horses and was known to gamble in other ways, too. By all accounts, James lost more than he won, and he soon became broke. Some believe he still longed for the notoriety he had years earlier. So, about the same time his daughter was born, James attempted to make a criminal comeback. To do so, he returned to a familiar place. He went back to Missouri.

Returning to a Life of Crime

Back in his home state, James recruited a group of common thieves to help him rob a train. On October 8, 1879, James and five other men rode into the small town of Glendale, Missouri. A Chicago and Alton Railroad train was scheduled to pass through the town. James and his novice helpers carried out plans similar to the way James's gangs had in the past. A couple of men rounded up all the villagers and took them hostage. Others piled rocks on the train tracks to force the train to stop. When it arrived at eight o'clock, the bandits jumped on board and robbed the train. They had expected it to be full of gold bullion. But, in the end, they rode off with only six thousand dollars cash.

The amount the bandits made from the robbery was far less than people were willing to pay to catch them. Still, no one did. James escaped back to his quiet life in

Tennessee. But the quiet life did not suit him for long. He was thirty-two years old and a restless outlaw at heart. Soon, he planned more robberies.

There was not as much time between these robberies as there had been before. In September 1880, James and his followers robbed a stagecoach at Mammoth Cave in Kentucky. The next month, they robbed a store in Mercer, Kentucky. Then they held up another stagecoach. On March 11, 1881, James was part of a gang that stole five thousand, two hundred dollars from a worker at the Muscle Shoals canal project in Alabama.[16] One of the bandits was arrested shortly after the robbery. When James learned of the arrest, he panicked. Surely, someone would soon connect him to the crime. Fearing he might be identified when and if his brother was, Frank James panicked, too. He did not want to leave his new life but felt he had to so he would not get caught. The James brothers sent their families away and left Tennessee for Kentucky. Soon, they all moved back to Missouri.

But by this time, Missouri governor Thomas Crittenden had teamed with the railroad companies to offer a large reward for the capture of the Jameses. It was five thousand dollars for each brother's capture, five thousand dollars for each one of them that was convicted, and five thousand dollars each for any other member of their gang. The governor asked citizens to rise against the brothers, "by day or night, until the entire band is either captured or exterminated."[17] Still, the daring brothers would rob again.

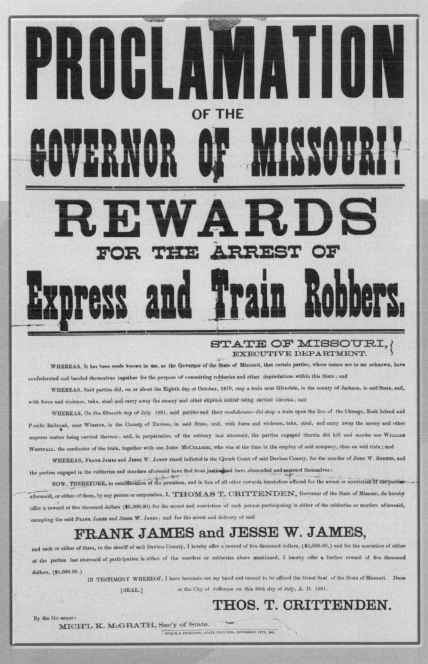

Missouri Governor Thomas Crittenden issued a proclamation for the arrest of Jesse and Frank James in 1881. He offered a reward of five thousand dollars.

Another Train Robbery

On July 15, 1881, the gang robbed the Chicago, Rock Island and Pacific Railroad at Winston, Missouri. One of the bandits shot and killed the train's conductor. Most historians believe it was Jesse James who killed him, though the motive and circumstances are unclear. A passenger was also killed. The bandits robbed the train's safe, but they only made off with about six hundred dollars.[18] The small amount of loot likely meant the bandits would rob again. On September 7, they did.

Exactly five years since their ruined robbery in Northfield, Minnesota, Frank and Jesse James found themselves in an area known as Blue Cut, Missouri. It was not a town, rather "a slice carved out of a thirty-foot hillside for the tracks of the Chicago and Alton Railroad."[19] The spot was near where the brothers had robbed a train two years before. The James brothers, and the rest of their gang piled rocks on the tracks a train was scheduled to pass over. When the train stopped, the robbers jumped aboard. All but one of the robbers was masked. The unmasked man had a beard and kept telling people he was Jesse James.[20] This time, the bandits even robbed the passengers. If they wanted to make off with any money, they pretty much had to, because the train's safe was nearly empty. When the bandits fled, the gang's leader, likely Jesse James, gave two silver dollars to the train's engineer. Then he said, "drink to the health of Jesse James."[21] Then the bandits were gone.

8

Fatal Plans

Jesse James's recent robberies were nowhere near as glamorous as his past ones had been. As the country moved on from its Civil War days, the James brothers had fewer and fewer supporters. Shortly after the war ended in 1865, many of the gang's supporters thought the members were just leftover bushwhackers fighting for the Southern cause by robbing from the rich Northerners. But now, more than fifteen years later, it was obvious to most that was not the case. Even newspaperman John Newman Edwards no longer wrote about the brothers. Nearly everyone felt Frank and Jesse James were only doing what they did to get money for themselves and not for any noble causes.

After the Blue Cut robbery, the James brothers again split up. Frank James moved his family to Lynchburg, Virginia. Jesse James, using the name Tom Howard at this time, moved his family into a rented house atop a hill in St. Joseph, Missouri. The city of St. Joseph was considered a good place for someone to hide. One report said: "The community bustled, and with travelers coming and going by the hundreds daily, it was easy for a person to get lost in the crowd."[1]

> But by 1881, many of the people James had run with had left the gang, been killed, or sent to jail.

The rent on James's hilltop home was fourteen dollars a month, and the house gave its occupants a good view of everything around it.[2] If bounty seekers approached the home, they would not be able to get inside without a fight. That is, unless they were considered friends. Charley and Bob Ford were just that. The brothers were new recruits into James's gang. In his early years of banditry, James had been a member of William Clarke Quantrill's Raiders, following Quantrill's orders. After Quantrill's death, he took more of a leadership role in selecting his own gang members. But by 1881, many of the people James had run with had left the gang, been killed, or sent to jail. Even his brother had retired from the criminal life.

Bob Ford, pictured here, met Jesse James in 1880.

If James wanted to continue robbing, he needed helpers. And the Ford brothers were willing.

The Ford Brothers

Born in Ray County, Missouri, the Fords grew up reading about the crazy capers of Jesse James and his gang. The Fords finally met Jesse in 1880, at a time when the legendary bandit was in dire need of new recruits. The Ford brothers soon became involved in James's gang. Charley Ford was believed to have participated in the train robbery at Blue Cut in 1881. But the younger Bob Ford most likely never took part in any robberies. His role with the gang was much smaller. He mostly performed odd jobs, similar to what James had done for Quantrill's Raiders before he was allowed to join that group.

So when the Fords showed up at their leader's home in March 1882, there appeared to be no reason for James to worry. In fact, the visit was scheduled. The three men were planning a bank robbery in Platte City, Missouri. This one, James said, was going to be his last. At thirty-four years old, he finally appeared to be growing weary of the outlaw game. After Platte City, he planned to move his family to Nebraska and retire on a farm.[3] No more worries, just a quiet life.

The plans of the Ford brothers would have been a big worry for James, if he had known about them. Their plans were simple: capture or kill James (depending on which story you believe) and take the reward money the governor had offered.

"The Ballad of Jesse James"

The last verse of the song most commonly known as "The Ballad of Jesse James" says it was written by a man named Billy Gashade. Many historians believe no one knows the tune's true author. The lyrics are not entirely accurate with James's life story, either. But many musicians still have performed it over the years, including superstar Bruce Springsteen. Each performance has helped perpetuate the myth that Jesse James was, like Robin Hood, a "friend to the poor." These are two verses from the song:

> Jesse James was a lad that killed a-many a man;
> He robbed the Danville train.
> But that dirty little coward that shot Mr. Howard
> Has laid poor Jesse in his grave.
>
> Jesse was a man, a friend to the poor,
> He never would see a man suffer pain;
> And with his brother Frank he robbed the Chicago bank,
> And stopped the Glendale train.[4]

Shot in the Back

After breakfast on April 3, the three men went over their plans for the Platte City robbery. Then the Fords put their own private plans into action. When James got up to straighten a picture on his wall, he turned his back to the Ford brothers. Bob Ford later told what happened next. He said, "Without further thought or a moment's delay I pulled my revolver and leveled it as I sat. He heard the hammer click as I cocked it with my thumb and started to turn as I pulled the trigger. The ball struck him just behind the ear and he fell like a log, dead."[5]

Zee James and her children were in the kitchen when Bob Ford shot Jesse James. When she heard the blast, she rushed to find out what happened. Charley Ford told her the gun went off on accident. But the grief-stricken wife did not believe him. In a book he wrote years later, Jesse Jr. related what he remembered about his father's murder, which happened when he was six years old. He said that "we had just finished break-fast. I heard from the front room the loud roar of a shot. My mother rushed in and screamed. I ran in after her and saw my father dead upon the floor, and my mother was down upon her knees by his side and was crying bitterly. . . . He never spoke or breathed after he fell."[6]

Word of James's death spread quickly. The excited Fords sent a telegraph to a few officials, including the governor, telling them what they had done. Both were taken to jail and charged with murder. Both pleaded guilty and the judge said they should be "taken to some

*Bob Ford murdered Jesse James in his home
in St. Joseph, Missouri, on April 3, 1882.*

convenient place and hanged by the neck until . . . dead."[7] But Governor Crittenden issued pardons for both men. They were set free. But the Fords never received the ten thousand dollars they had expected. In the end, they received only about five hundred dollars for expenses.[8]

News of James's Death

The first newspaper article on James's death ran in the April 4 edition of the *Kansas City Times*. It read: "The home where the great outlaw was killed is a frame building, a story and a half high, sitting in a little grove of fruit trees on one of the round ridges back of the World's hotel. It commands a view of the approaches for a long distance."[9] The story went on to talk about how the Fords had confessed and gave an account of Zee James's reaction to her husband's death. "My husband is Jesse James, and a kinder hearted, truer man to his family never lived," she told the writer.[10] The journalist added his own spin on the story. He wrote, "The thought that Jesse James has lived among us for the past six months, and walked our streets daily, causes one to shudder with fear."[11]

Locals may have been fearful of James, but they all were not happy with the Fords. Shooting someone in the back was considered a cowardly deed. Many people wanted the Ford brothers to pay for what they had done. Eventually, they did, but it was not authorities that made them do so. Charley Ford lived a life on the run for a little more than two years. On May 4, 1884, he committed suicide. Ten years after Bob Ford killed Jesse James, he suffered a similar fate. On June 8, 1892, Edward O'Kelley shot and killed Ford in Colorado. Later, O'Kelley was also murdered.

> **"There was never a more cowardly and unnecessary murder committed in all of America than this murder of Jesse James."**

Newspapers reported on James's murder nonstop. James sympathizer, John Newman Edwards, even chimed in. He called both Ford brothers cowards in an editorial published in a Missouri newspaper. He wrote, "There was never a more cowardly and unnecessary murder committed in all of America than this murder of Jesse James."[12]

Burial at the James Farm

James's funeral was held April 6, in Kearney, Missouri. Two thousand people attended.[13] Many of them just wanted to get a look at the notorious outlaw they had heard and read so much about. James's mother was still upset over what had been done to her son. She said, "my son has gone to God, but his friends still live and will have revenge on those who murdered him for money."[14]

James was buried in the front yard of the family farm. Only close friends and relatives were there. His mother had a marker made for his grave. It read: "In Loving Remembrance of My Beloved Son: Jesse James. Died April 3, 1882. Aged 34 years, 6 months, 28 days. Murdered by a Traitor and Coward Whose Name is Not

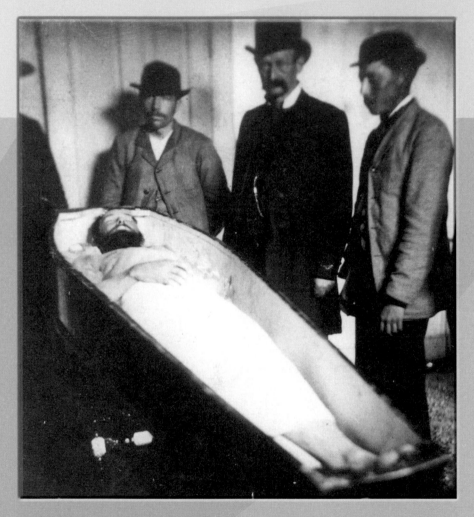

Stories about Jesse James's death spread around the United States. This photo shows his body in a coffin before his burial.

Worthy to Appear Here."[15] Zee also auctioned off James's belongings to pay for expenses. She raised $117, and sold James's dog, Boo, for five dollars.[16] Some stories say James's mother even considered accepting a ten-thousand-dollar offer for her son's body from a promoter who wanted to put it on ice and take it on a tour across the country.[17]

Frank James Turns Himself In

Frank James did not attend either of his brother's memorial services. He did not find out about his brother's death until a couple days after it happened. Like most people, he read about it in a newspaper. He said, "My God, where and how and who killed him?"[18] For a long while, the older brother had sought a quieter life. Now, he no longer wanted to hide from the law. On October 5, 1882, James surrendered to Governor Crittenden. He said, "I'm tired of running . . . tired of waiting for a ball in the back. Tired of looking into the faces of friends and seeing a Judas."[19]

Frank James was taken by train to Independence, Missouri. Crowds gathered at various points along the route, hoping to catch a glimpse of the famous bandit. A large number of the onlookers gave him a hero's welcome. When he arrived in Independence, James was placed in jail. He eventually stood trial twice. Each of the two juries acquitted him. Years later, James talked about his situation. He said, "I am not as bad as I have been painted; for beneath the ugly caricatures unjustly given of me by the public press, I beg to assure you that

Two thousand people attended the funeral of Jesse James. This photo shows the room in which James was killed in St. Joseph, Missouri.

there beats a heart of truth, kindness, love for my fellow man, and loyalty to society."[20]

Finally free, Frank James moved around a bit and worked various jobs. He sold shoes, worked at a dry-goods store, and acted as starter for horse races at county fairs. His celebrity made him a popular attraction wherever he went. At the dry-goods store, it was said that "the women flock about him to buy dry goods. . . . It's Mr. James this and Mr. James that . . . [though not] all the women visit him at the store and dote upon him, but a big per cent of them do."[21] The death of Jesse James finally allowed his brother to live a more normal life. That is, as normal as a famous ex-outlaw could.

The Legend Lives

D ozens of photographs were taken of Jesse James's body after he was killed. They show scars from wounds he had suffered in shootouts. The coroner's jury reported, "We the jury find that the deceased is Jesse James, and that he came to his death by a shot from a pistol in the hands of Robert Ford."[1] Even James's mom, Zerelda Samuel, identified the dead person as her son. She said, "Would to God that it were not!"[2]

Jesse James Imposters

Yet some people still were not convinced that James had died. They believed his death was a hoax. Some even believed he faked his own death, so he could finally be free from the law. These theories would pop up several times over the next few decades. Several Jesse James imposters emerged over the years. One of the best known was a man who called himself John James.

John James had spent time in prison for killing a man. He knew enough about the real Jesse James that he was able to fool some people for a while. He said he had faked his own death so he could leave his banditry behind and settle with his family on a Nebraska farm. That is what the real Jesse James had said he wanted to do. John James began making appearances at various cities in the Midwest. But his gig was soon up.

At one of John James's appearances, a lady in the crowd shouted out at him. It was Stella James, wife of Jesse Jr. She had one of Jesse James's boots and asked John James to try it on. It did not fit, offering proof he was not Jesse James. John James died in an Arkansas mental hospital in 1947.[3]

Around the time John James died, another high-profile imposter emerged. It was an Oklahoma man named J. Frank Dalton, who said he was one hundred years old, the same age Jesse James would have been. Dalton's act went on for a couple of years. He made appearances at carnivals and parades. In 1950, he even appeared in a national radio broadcast on the NBC network. Newspapers and books were written about him.

Dalton took his tale with him to his grave. When he died, his tombstone said: "Jesse Woodson James, Sept. 5, 1847–August 15, 1951. Supposedly killed in 1882."[4] Dalton's claims repeatedly have been proven untrue, and many of his stories were considered ridiculous.

Over the years, there have been more Jesse James imposters. But those who believed Jesse James was not the one killed by Bob Ford were definitely in the minority. In Missouri and elsewhere most believed James had died. His legend, however, never has.

Spreading the Legend of Jesse James

At the time of James's death, so-called dime novels were a popular form of entertainment for Americans. The small books were filled with exciting stories. They were fast-paced and thrilling. Several of them were written about the James brothers. Titles included *The Train Robbers, or A Story of the James Boys*; *The James Boys as Guerillas*; and *The James Boys in Mexico*. Most of the books were highly sensational. All of them were exaggerated. They were filled with dialogue between Frank James, Jesse James, and others that never happened. For example, in one book called *Jesse James, the Outlaw*, the author shows the brothers taking part in a holdup that never occurred:

> *"Throw up your hands, curse you!" thundered Jesse James, with a terrible oath, covering us with his revolver, as we all came to a startled halt.*

Dime novels were a popular form of entertainment when Jesse James died. These books created sensational views of Jesse James and led to other productions about the life and legend of James.

His companions did the same, while motioning me to one side, as a person too insignificant to be mixed up in the quarrel.

"Throw up your hands," echoed Frank James, in an equally unmistakable tone.

Paralyzed with sudden panic, Jewell and Whittaker obeyed at once.

Hawes, however, saw that the game was up, surrender or no surrender. He resolved to die hard, if die he must.

"Not if I know it!" he growled, whipping out his revolver and firing with the rapidity of thought.

*His bullet passed through the neck of the James'
confederate—a train-robber, named Curly Pitts—
who thereupon tumbled from the saddle, after
firing his own pistol in the air.*

*At the same instant Hawes fell dead, with Jesse
James' bullet in his heart.*[5]

Thousands of people read each dime novel. Many
believed the tales were true. Jesse James's mother said
they were not. She said, "I read them all and they're
awful. . . . There ought to be a law against printing such
stuff."[6]

Some who had read the dime novels admired James
and copied aspects of his life. Charles Arthur "Pretty
Boy" Floyd was one of them. Like Jesse James, the
Oklahoma man also robbed banks. Floyd also grabbed
hold of Jesse James's Robin Hood image of only robbing
from the rich. He once wrote, "I have robbed no one but
the monied men."[7] That was not true with Jesse James
and it was not true with Floyd. As they had been for the
James brothers, rewards were offered for Floyd. He was
shot and killed by authorities in Ohio in 1934. Floyd
has been made the subject of several books and several
movies. He even was the subject of a song written by
folk singer Woody Guthrie.

Most people did not take their fascination with Jesse
James as far as "Pretty Boy" Floyd did. But many did
want to visit the place where the legend lived. Zerelda
Samuel turned their visits to the farm into a business.
She charged tourists a fee to come inside the home. She
told stories while they were there. People flocked to the

Jesse James Legend: Fact or Fiction?

Dime novels helped keep the legend of Jesse James alive, but they also helped spread false information about the outlaw's life. Through the years, several credible authors have pored over thousands of newspaper articles, official documents, books, letters, and numerous other sources of information in their attempts to paint a truthful and accurate picture of the lives of Frank and Jesse James. In his well-regarded 1966 book, *Jesse James Was His Name*, William A. Settle Jr. talked about his struggles in uncovering the truth about the James brothers. He wrote: "Their exploits were indeed real; their crimes are of public record. The legend, however, is a different matter. In it fact and fiction are so entwined that it is difficult—at times, impossible—to untangle them."[8]

farm to see it and the other attractions. Those who were willing to pay more could leave with a souvenir, such as some stones from James's grave.

When Jesse James's wife, Zee, died in 1900, she was buried in the Mount Olivet Cemetery in Kearney, Missouri. Two years later, Jesse James's remains were removed from their burial site on the family farm and buried next to his wife.

Fate of the Youngers

In 1889, thirty-four-year-old Bob Younger died in prison of what then was called consumption and today is known as tuberculosis. In 1901, his brothers, Cole and Jim, were released from prison after more than twenty-five years. Both men were in their fifties. The brothers went to work as salesmen for a Minnesota company that made tombstones. Jim Younger struggled with living in the outside world and with his health. On October 19, 1902, he committed suicide. Cole Younger returned to Missouri and soon got back in touch with Frank James. The two men were the only surviving members of the James-Younger gang. In 1903, they teamed up to create the Great Cole Younger and Frank James Historical Wild West show. The show featured "American Cowboys, Roosevelt Rough Riders, Indians, Cubans, Western Girls, Mexicans, Broncos" and more.[9] It toured to several cities but often received poor reviews. One read: "The show is generally regarded as being without exception the poorest one ever seen in this city."[10] The show also made little money. Overall, it was a disaster and ended less than a year after it began. Younger worked various jobs, including giving lectures, until he died in 1916, at the age of seventy-two.

When his mother died in 1911, Frank James moved back to the James farm. He took over the tourist business his mother had started. For four years, he charged visitors fifty cents each to tour the legendary site. He was seventy-two years old when he died in 1915. After his death, three separate men—one in Moccasin Bend, Tennessee; one in Tacoma, Washington; and one in Wayton, Arkansas—claimed to be Frank James.[11]

In 1978, Clay County bought the James farm and restored it. To this day, the farm remains a popular tourist attraction. The place where Jesse James was born and his brother Frank died is called the James Farm and Museum. Several events are held there each year. Many people even believe it is haunted.

Memorials to Jesse James

There are many other Jesse James museums and attractions. The St. Joseph, Missouri, home he was killed in draws thousands of visitors each year. In the 1930s, the house was moved from its original site to a more central location. The home is a museum and features James's coffin handles and the bullet that had almost killed him when he was shot trying to surrender at Lexington, Kentucky, in 1865. Both the bullet and the coffin handles were taken from James's grave when it was exhumed in 1995. The home also features a hole in the wall supposedly made by the bullet that killed James.

Frank James, at age seventy, stands in front of the gate at the James farm. He died in 1915 at the age of seventy-two.

As it turns out, it is not really a bullet hole, though it had long been reported to be. Today, historians believe the bullet that killed James never left his head.

The Jesse James Bank Museum is located in Liberty, Missouri. It is the former home of the Clay County Savings Bank, which was robbed of almost sixty thousand dollars in February 1866. It is commonly believed that Jesse James was not even part of the robbery, yet the building bears his name. It is open six days a week and costs $5.50 to enter.

Every year, the city of Northfield, Minnesota, holds a celebration called The Defeat of Jesse James Days. Activities include parades, fireworks, and dancing. The main event is a reenactment of the failed 1876 bank raid conducted by the James brothers and the Younger brothers.

James's hometown of Kearney, Missouri, holds a celebration each September called the Jesse James Festival. The celebration features a carnival, a parade, a rodeo, and reenactments of historic events. Many of the activities are held at Jesse James Park.

The legend of Jesse James still provides entertainment. Singers reference his name in songs. His name often appears in TV shows. New books are being written, and numerous films have been made about him. In 2007, actor Brad Pitt played Jesse James in the movie *The Assassination of Jesse James by the Coward Robert Ford*. Jesse Jr. even starred as his father in two films: *Jesse James Under the Black Flag* and *Jesse James as the Outlaw* in 1921. In 1966, there was a film called *Jesse James Meets Frankenstein's Daughter*.

Jesse Jr. wrote a book about his dad in 1899. It was called, *Jesse James, My Father*. In it, the outlaw's son said he had read hundreds of other stories about his dad, and many of them were entirely wrong. He also said he has never seen his father "credited with having in his nature any of the human attributes of kindness, charity or honesty of purpose. In all of these writings his true character is entirely lost sight of and distorted into that of a veritable Frankenstein who slew mercilessly and robbed for the mere love of adventure."[12] The son also defended his father's kind heart. He wrote: "I defy the world to show that he ever slew a human being except in the protection of his own life or as a soldier in honorable warfare. . . . There were lovable and noble traits in the

Numerous films and TV shows have been made about Jesse James. Actor Brad Pitt (left) played the role of James in the 2007 film The Assassination of Jesse James by the Coward Robert Ford.

character of my father. . . . "[13] Jesse Jr. became a lawyer and died in 1951.

Modern science has entered into the Jesse James story. On July 18, 1995, James's grave at the Mount Olivet Cemetery was dug up. Scientists tested the grave's remains and compared their DNA with DNA from descendants of James's sister. The testing proved that the remains belonged to Jesse James. All the years of imposters had been just that. The real Jesse James had been killed by Robert Ford, just as most believed he had been. In addition to finding the bullet from 1865 and the coffin handles among the remains, scientists also found a diamond-shaped tiepin, took a cast of

Imposters claimed to be Jesse James long after his death. In July 1995, DNA testing proved Jesse James had been killed by Robert Ford. Above, workers dig up the grave of James at the Mount Olivet Cemetery in Kearney, Missouri.

James's skull that showed where the bullet entered, and made castings of ten of James's teeth.

James Starrs, a scientist from George Washington University in Washington, D.C., led the exhumation. Starrs concluded, "As far as I am concerned and the individual members of my team, there is no lack of certainty that we have identified the remains as being those of Jesse James. The hair, and the teeth and the known relatives all matched."[14] Despite the scientific evidence, a small group of people still dispute the findings, saying they were flawed.

> **The testing proved that the remains belonged to Jesse James.**

Today, a sign near the town of Gads Hill, Missouri, marks the state's first-ever train robbery. It reads: "Gads Hill Train Robbery. Jesse James with four members of his band carried out the first Missouri train robbery here January 31, 1874."

Was the real Jesse James the man who robbed from the rich and gave to the poor, as his actions at the Gads Hill robbery might suggest? Or was the real Jesse James the man who took part in the merciless killing of two dozen unarmed soldiers during a train robbery in Centralia, Missouri? Most believe the latter, yet that debate is likely to continue. However, one fact is not debatable. Jesse James is a legend and a large part of the folklore of America's Wild West. It is unlikely that legend—unlike the man himself—will ever die.

CHRONOLOGY

1843 — Alexander Franklin "Frank" James born January 10 in Clay County, Missouri.

1844 — Thomas Coleman "Cole" Younger born in Clay County, Missouri.

1847 — Jesse Woodson James born September 5 in Clay County, Missouri.

1850 — Robert Sallee James dies of fever in Placerville, California.

1861 — Civil War begins; Frank James joins the Confederate Army.

1862 — Union soldiers capture Frank James.

1863 — Frank James joins William Clarke Quantrill's Raiders; Lawrence massacre takes place; General Orders No. 11 enacted.

1864 — Jesse James joins Quantrill's Raiders, participates in raid on Centralia, Missouri; Jesse James is shot for the first time.

1865 — Civil War ends; President Abraham Lincoln is assassinated; William Clarke Quantrill dies.

1866 — Jesse James is shot in the chest; bandits rob Clay County Savings Bank; James participates in robbery of Alexander Mitchell and Company bank in Lexington, Missouri.

1868—James-Younger gang robs The Bank of Nimrod L. Long and Company in Russellville, Kentucky.

1869—Jesse and Frank James participate in robbery of the Daviess County Savings Bank in Gallatin, Missouri, killing banker John W. Sheets in the process.

1871—James-Younger gang robs the Ocobock Brothers bank in Corydon, Iowa; Allan Pinkerton's National Detective Agency is hired to catch the bandits.

1872—James-Younger gang robs the Bank of Columbia in Columbia, Kentucky, killing cashier R. A. C. Martin in the process; James brothers participate in robbery at the Kansas City fair.

1873—James-Younger gang robs the Ste. Genevieve Savings Association in Ste. Genevieve, Missouri; James-Younger gang robs the Chicago, Rock Island and Pacific Railroad at Adair, Iowa, its first train robbery.

1874—James-Younger gang robs stagecoach near Hot Springs, Arkansas; gang robs train at Gads Hill, Missouri; John Younger shot and killed by Pinkerton agent; Jesse James marries Zerelda "Zee" Mimms; Frank James marries Annie Ralston; James-Younger gang robs train in Muncie, Kansas.

1875—Pinkerton agents raid James farm, wounding Jesse and Frank James's mother and killing their eight-year-old half-brother; Jesse Edwards James born; Jesse James begins using alias, John Davis Howard.

1876 —James-Younger gang robs Missouri Pacific Railroad train in Rocky Cut, Missouri, and First National Bank in Northfield, Minnesota; Younger brothers captured.

1878 —Robert Franklin James born to Frank and Annie James.

1879 —Mary Susan James born to Jesse and Zee James; Jesse James leads group of men in robbery of the Chicago and Alton Railroad in Glendale, Missouri.

1880 —Jesse James and his gang commit several small-scale robberies.

1881 —Missouri Governor Thomas Crittenden offers a reward for capture of the James brothers; Jesse James and his gang rob a worker at the Muscle Shoals canal project in Alabama; James gang robs the Chicago, Rock Island and Pacific Railroad at Winston, Missouri, killing the train's conductor and a passenger; James gang robs a train at Blue Cut, Missouri.

1882 —Bob Ford shoots and kills Jesse James at James's home in St. Joseph, Missouri; Frank James surrenders to authorities.

1892 —Bob Ford shot and killed in Colorado.

1900 —Zee James dies.

1915 —Frank James dies.

1916 —Cole Younger dies.

CHAPTER NOTES

CHAPTER 1
"The Most Daring Robbery on Record"

1. T. J. Stiles, *Jesse James: Last Rebel of the Civil War* (New York: Alfred A. Knopf, 2002), p. 243.
2. Ronald H. Beights, "Jesse James and the Gads Hill Train Holdup," Wild West, June 2005, <http://www.historynet .com/magazines/wild_west/3034996.html> (October 31, 2007).
3. Stiles, p. 244.
4. Beights, "Jesse James and the Gads Hill Train Holdup."
5. Ted P. Yeatman, *Frank and Jesse James: The Story Behind the Legend* (Nashville, Tenn.: Cumberland House, 2000), p. 21.
6. *The Gunfighters* (Alexandria, Va.: Time-Life Books, 1974), p. 67.
7. Ibid.
8. Beights, "Jesse James and the Gads Hill Train Holdup."

CHAPTER 2
War at the Border and Beyond

1. Phillip W. Steele, *The Many Faces of Jesse James* (Gretna, La.: Pelican Publishing Company, 1995), p. 17.
2. "Distinctives: A Brief History of Jewell," The Jewel Journey, n.d., <http://www.jewell.edu/william_jewell/gen/william_ and_jewell_generated_pages/A_Brief_History_m21.html> (November 2, 2007).
3. William A. Settle Jr., *Jesse James Was His Name* (Lincoln, Nebr.: University of Nebraska Press, 1966), p. 7.
4. Ibid.
5. Ibid.
6. Robertus Love, *The Rise and Fall of Jesse James* (Lincoln, Nebr.: University of Nebraska Press, 1990), p. 33.
7. Settle, p. 8.

8. Love, p. 34.
9. Homer Croy, *Jesse James Was My Neighbor* (New York: Duell, Sloan and Pearce, 1949), p. 20.
10. Settle, p. 9.
11. Love, p. 36.
12. Ibid., p. 29.
13. Ibid.
14. T. J. Stiles, *Jesse James: Last Rebel of the Civil War* (New York: Alfred A. Knopf, 2002), p. 63.
15. Ibid., p. 67.
16. Ibid., p. 77.
17. Duane Schultz, *Quantrill's War: The Life and Times of William Clarke Quantrill* (New York: St. Martin's Press, 1996), p. 2.
18. Ibid.
19. Ted P. Yeatman, *Frank and Jesse James: The Story Behind the Legend* (Nashville, Tenn.: Cumberland House, 2000), p. 35.
20. Marley Brant, *The Outlaw Youngers: A Confederate Brotherhood* (Lanham, Md.: Madison Books, 1992), pp. 29–30.
21. Yeatman, p. 41.
22. Steele, p. 24.
23. Settle, p. 26.
24. Stiles, p. 89.
25. Ibid.
26. Yeatman, p. 40.

CHAPTER 3

Raiders on the Rampage

1. Michael Fellman, *Inside War: The Guerrilla Conflict in Missouri During the Civil War* (Oxford University Press, USA, 1990), p. 25.
2. Ibid.
3. Duane Schultz, *Quantrill's War: The Life and Times of William Clarke Quantrill* (New York: St. Martin's Press, 1996), p. 171.
4. "The Lawrence Massacre by a Band of Missouri Ruffians Under Quantrell," Americancivilwar.com, June 30, 1994, <http://americancivilwar.com/documents/quantrel_raid.html> (December 11, 2007).
5. "The Eldridge: History," The Eldridge, 2007, <http://eldridgehotel.com/hotel_history.htm> (March 10, 2008).

6. Kathy Weiser, "Eldridge Hotel: History and Hauntings," Legends of America, 2008, <http://www.legendsofamerica.com/OZ-EldridgeHotel.html> (March 10, 2008).
7. Albert Castel, "Order No. 11 and the Civil War on the Border," Civil War St. Louis, 1963–2003, <www.civilwarstlouis.com/History2/castelorder11.htm> (December 12, 2007).
8. Schultz, p. 244.
9. Ibid.
10. Castel, "Order No. 11 and the Civil War on the Border."
11. Ted P. Yeatman, *Frank and Jesse James: The Story Behind the Legend* (Nashville, Tenn.: Cumberland House, 2000), p. 47.
12. Ibid.
13. Fellman, p. 104.
14. William A. Settle Jr., *Jesse James Was His Name* (Lincoln, Nebr.: University of Nebraska Press, 1966), p. 27.
15. Ibid.
16. Fellman, p. 188.
17. "The Centralia Massacre and Battle: September 27, 1864," Mid-Missouri Civil War Round Table, n.d., <http://mmcwrt.missouri.org/2000/default0007.htm> (December 20, 2007).
18. Ibid.
19. Yeatman, p. 58.
20. Ibid., p. 71.
21. T. J. Stiles, *Jesse James: Last Rebel of the Civil War* (New York: Alfred A. Knopf, 2002), p. 153.
22. Ibid.
23. John Newman Edwards, *A Terrible Quintette*, reproduced at *The Paper*, November 10, 2005, <http://www.thecommunitypaper.com/2005/11_10_05/coverstory.php> (March 10, 2008).
24. Yeatman, p. 375.

CHAPTER 4
Becoming Bandits

1. John Newman Edwards, *A Terrible Quintette*, reproduced at *The Paper*, November 10, 2005, <http://www.thecommunitypaper.com/2005/11_10_05/coverstory.php> (March 10, 2008).

2. William A. Settle Jr., *Jesse James Was His Name* (Lincoln, Nebr.: University of Nebraska Press, 1966), p. 33.
3. Ted P. Yeatman, *Frank and Jesse James: The Story Behind the Legend* (Nashville, Tennessee: Cumberland House, 2000), p. 87.
4. Marley Brant, *The Outlaw Youngers: A Confederate Brotherhood* (Lanham, Md.: Madison Books, 1992), p. 74.
5. Edwards.
6. Ibid.
7. T. J. Stiles, *Jesse James: Last Rebel of the Civil War* (New York: Alfred A. Knopf, 2002), p. 174.
8. Yeatman, p. 91.
9. Ibid.
10. Ibid., p. 93.
11. Ibid.
12. Stiles, p. 197.
13. Ibid.
14. Settle, p. 35.
15. Stiles, p. 197.
16. Brant, p. 84.
17. Settle, p. 38.
18. Brant, p. 88.
19. Settle, p. 40.
20. Yeatman, p. 97.
21. Ibid.
22. Ibid., p. 98.
23. Ibid.
24. Settle, p. 41.
25. "An Outlaw's Arsenal," *American Experience: Jesse James*, PBS.org, 2005, <http://www.pbs.org/wgbh/amex/james/peopleevents/e_guns.html> (October 3, 2008).
26. Ibid.
27. Ibid.
28. Roger A. Bruns, *The Bandit Kings: From Jesse James to Pretty Boy Floyd* (New York: Crown Publishers, Inc., 1995), p. 34.

CHAPTER 5
The Robberies Continue

1. Ted P. Yeatman, *Frank and Jesse James: The Story Behind the Legend* (Nashville, Tenn.: Cumberland House, 2000), p. 99.

2. Ibid., p. 100.
3. Marley Brant, *The Outlaw Youngers: A Confederate Brotherhood* (Lanham, Md.: Madison Books, 1992), p. 106.
4. Ibid., p. 111.
5. William A. Settle Jr., *Jesse James Was His Name* (Lincoln, Nebr.: University of Nebraska Press, 1966), p. 45.
6. T. J. Stiles, *Jesse James: Last Rebel of the Civil War* (New York: Alfred A. Knopf, 2002), p. 223.
7. Settle, p. 45.
8. Ibid., p. 46.
9. Stiles, pp. 224–225.
10. Settle, p. 47.
11. Stiles, p. 228.
12. Brant, p. 116.
13. Yeatman, pp. 106–107.
14. Donald L. Gilmore, "When the James Gang Ruled the Rails," HistoryNet.com, 2008, <http://www.historynet .com/magazines/wild_west/3025691.html?page=1&c=y> (February 11, 2008).
15. "Old West Legends: Timeline of the James Gang," Legends ofAmerica.com, 2008, <http://www.legendsofamerica.com/ WE-JesseJamesTimeline8.html> (February 11, 2008).
16. *The Gunfighters* (Alexandria, Va.: Time-Life Books, 1974), p. 67.
17. Ibid.

CHAPTER 6
Family Life

1. *The Gunfighters* (Alexandria, Va.: Time-Life Books, 1974), p. 68.
2. Phillip W. Steele, *The Many Faces of Jesse James* (Gretna, La.: Pelican Publishing Company, 1995), p. 45.
3. T. J. Stiles, *Jesse James: Last Rebel of the Civil War* (New York: Alfred A. Knopf, 2002), p. 259.
4. Kathy Weiser, "Zee James: Jesse's 'Poor' Wife," Legends of America, 2008, <http://www.legendsofamerica.com/WE-ZeeJames.html> (January 14, 2008).
5. Stiles, p. 273.
6. Ibid., p. 275.

7. William A. Settle Jr., *Jesse James Was His Name* (Lincoln, Nebr.: University of Nebraska Press, 1966), p. 75.
8. Stiles, p. 301.
9. Ted P. Yeatman, *Frank and Jesse James: The Story Behind the Legend* (Nashville, Tenn.: Cumberland House, 2000), p. 136.
10. Settle, pp. 77–78.
11. Ibid.
12. Ibid., p. 78.
13. Marley Brant, *The Outlaw Youngers: A Confederate Brotherhood* (Lanham, Md.: Madison Books, 1992), p. 156.
14. Ibid., p. 158.
15. Stiles, p. 298.
16. *The Gunfighters*, p. 72.

CHAPTER 7
"Get Your Guns, Boys!"

1. Marley Brant, *The Outlaw Youngers: A Confederate Brotherhood* (Lanham, Md.: Madison Books, 1992), p. 170.
2. Ted P. Yeatman, *Frank and Jesse James: The Story Behind the Legend* (Nashville, Tenn.: Cumberland House, 2000), p. 173.
3. T. J. Stiles, *Jesse James: Last Rebel of the Civil War* (New York: Alfred A. Knopf, 2002), p. 334.
4. Brant, p. 182.
5. Ibid., p 184.
6. Yeatman, p. 175.
7. Ibid., p. 178.
8. "James and Youngers: The Northfield, Minnesota Robbery," Civil War St. Louis, 2001–2007, <http://www.civilwar stlouis.com/History/jamesnorthfield.htm> (January 15, 2008).
9. Allen Barra, "Jesse James: Last Rebel of the Civil War" book review, Salon.com, n.d., <http://dir.salon.com/story/books/review/2002/10/15/stiles/index1.html> (September 20, 2008).
10. *The Gunfighters* (Alexandria, Va.: Time-Life Books, 1974), p. 80.
11. Stiles, p. 346.
12. Brant, p. 203.
13. Kathy Weiser, "Jesse James: Folklore Hero or Cold-Blooded Hero?," Legends of America, 2003–2008, <http://www.

legendsofamerica.com/WE-JesseJames7.html> (January 14, 2008).

14. Stiles, p. 351.

15. Ibid.

16. "Old West Legends: Timeline of the James Gang," Legends ofAmerica.com, 2008, <http://www.legendsofamerica.com/ WE-JesseJamesTimeline8.html> (February 18, 2008).

17. Roger A. Bruns, *The Bandit Kings: From Jesse James to Pretty Boy Floyd* (New York: Crown Publishers, Inc., 1995), p. 47.

18. Stiles, p. 364.

19. Richard Patterson, *Historical Atlas of the Outlaw West* (Boulder, Colo.: Johnson Books, 1985), p. 81.

20. Ibid.

21. Ibid.

CHAPTER 8
Fatal Plans

1. Richard Patterson, *Historical Atlas of the Outlaw West* (Boulder, Colo.: Johnson Books, 1985), p. 89.

2. Marley Brant, *The Outlaw Youngers: A Confederate Brotherhood* (Lanham, Md.: Madison Books, 1992), p. 222.

3. Roger A. Bruns, *The Bandit Kings: From Jesse James to Pretty Boy Floyd* (New York: Crown Publishers, Inc., 1995), p. 47.

4. "Jesse James," Project Gutenberg, May 4, 2007, <http:// www.gutenberg.org/files/21300/21300-8.txt> (February 28, 2008).

5. *The Gunfighters* (Alexandria, Va.: Time-Life Books, 1974), p. 80.

6. Jesse James Jr., "Jesse James, My Father," reprinted at Civil War St. Louis, 2001–2007, <http://www.civilwarstlouis .com/History/jamesgangjessejr1.htm> (January 12, 2008).

7. Ted P. Yeatman, *Frank and Jesse James: The Story Behind the Legend* (Nashville, Tenn.: Cumberland House, 2000), p. 275.

8. Brant, p. 224.

9. David Dary, *Red Blood and Black Ink: Journalism in the Old West* (New York: Alfred A. Knopf, 1998), p. 177.

10. Ibid., p. 181.

11. Ibid.

12. Yeatman, p. 346.

13. T. J. Stiles, *Jesse James: Last Rebel of the Civil War* (New York: Alfred A. Knopf, 2002), p. 377.
14. William A. Settle Jr., *Jesse James Was His Name* (Lincoln, Nebr.: University of Nebraska Press, 1966), p. 119.
15. Dale L. Walker, *Legends and Lies: Great Mysteries of the American West* (New York: Tom Doherty Associates, 1997), p. 99.
16. Brant, p. 224.
17. Transcript, *American Experience: Jesse James*, PBS.org, 2005, <http://www.pbs.org/wgbh/amex/james/filmmore/pt.html> (October 3, 2008).
18. Yeatman, p. 270.
19. Duane Schultz, *Quantrill's War: The Life and Times of William Clarke Quantrill* (New York: St. Martin's Press, 1996), p. 305.
20. Yeatman, p. 367.
21. Ibid., p. 290.

CHAPTER 9
The Legend Lives

1. William A. Settle Jr., *Jesse James Was His Name* (Lincoln, Nebr.: University of Nebraska Press, 1966), p. 118.
2. Ibid., p. 119.
3. Dale L. Walker, *Legends and Lies: Great Mysteries of the American West* (New York: Tom Doherty Associates, 1997), p. 101.
4. Ibid., p. 105.
5. W. B. Lawson, *Jesse James, The Outlaw: A Narrative of the James Boys* (New York: Street and Smith, 2001), <http://www-sul.stanford.edu/depts/dp/pennies/texts/204.html> (February 29, 2008).
6. Ted P. Yeatman, *Frank and Jesse James: The Story Behind the Legend* (Nashville, Tenn.: Cumberland House, 2000), p. 297.
7. Roger A. Bruns, *The Bandit Kings: From Jesse James to Pretty Boy Floyd* (New York: Crown Publishers, Inc., 1995), p. 224.
8. Settle, p. 2.
9. Marley Brant, *The Outlaw Youngers: A Confederate Brotherhood* (Lanham, Md.: Madison Books, 1992), p. 222.
10. Yeatman, p. 310.
11. Phillip W. Steele, *The Many Faces of Jesse James* (Gretna, La.: Pelican Publishing Company, 1995) p. 98.

12. Jesse James Jr., "Jesse James, My Father," reprinted at Civil War St. Louis, 2001–2007, <http://www.civilwarstlouis .com/History/jamesgangjessejr1.htm> (January 12, 2008).
13. Ibid.
14. SoundVision Productions, "The DNA Files: Law and the Genetics of Identity," 1998, <http://www.dnafiles.org/node/ 554> (October 10, 2008).

GLOSSARY

alibi—A form of defense that places a person somewhere other than the place where a crime was committed.

bushwhacker—A person who engages in guerrilla fighting.

Confederacy—A group of Southern states that seceded from the United States between 1860 and 1861. Also often referred to as the South.

DNA—Short for deoxyribonucleic acid; the material that transfers genetic characteristics from one life form to another.

free state—A state in which slavery was not allowed.

guerrilla—A fighter, usually part of a small group, that engages in irregular warfare often by using sabotage and harassment.

jayhawker—An antislavery guerrilla of Missouri and Kansas during the Civil War years.

peacetime—A time where no war is taking place.

popular sovereignty—The idea that the people living in a particular area should make their own laws.

symbolic—Something that stands for or represents something else.

telegraph—A device that converts a coded message into electric impulses and sends it through wires to distant places.

Union—Name for the proslavery states that did not secede from the United States during the Civil War. Also often referred to as the North.

widow—A woman who has outlived the man to whom she was married at the time of his death.

FURTHER READING

Blackwood, Gary L. *Outlaws.* New York: Benchmark Books, 2002.

Frisch, Aaron. *Jesse James.* Mankato, Minn.: Creative Education, 2006.

Randolph, Ryan. *A Bank Robber's End: The Death of Jesse James.* New York: Rosen Pub. Group, 2004.

Robinson, J. Dennis. *Jesse James: Legendary Rebel and Outlaw.* Minneapolis, Minn.: Compass Point Books, 2007.

Saffer, Barbara. *Jesse James.* Philadelphia: Chelsea House Publishers, 2002.

INTERNET ADDRESSES

Awesome Stories: Jesse James
<http://www.awesomestories.com/flicks/
jesse-james/summary>

Friends of the James Farm
<http://www.jessejames.org>

Legends of America: Jesse James—Folklore Hero or
Cold Blooded Killer?
<http://www.legendsofamerica.com/
WE-JesseJames.html>

INDEX

Miller, Clell, 52, 72, 74
Missouri Pacific Railroad
    robbery, 72
murders, 47, 55, 58, 63–64, 74,
    76, 80, 84
Muscle Shoals canal project
    robbery, 82

O

Ocobock Brothers bank robbery,
    52–55
O'Kelley, Edward, 93

P

Pinkerton, Allan, 8, 54
Pinkerton's National Detective
    Agency, 52, 54, 59, 63–64,
    67–70, 72
Pitts, Charlie, 72, 74, 76, 79, 80

Q

Quantrill, William Clarke, 20–
    22, 32, 36–37, 40–41, 86
Quantrill's Raiders, 22, 24–25,
    27–37, 86, 88

R

Reno, John/Simeon, 59
robberies
    banks, 41–48, 52–58, 61, 74–
        79, 105, 109
    overview, 80
    stagecoaches, 35, 61–62, 82
    trains, 5–10, 35, 58–59, 65–
        67, 72, 81–82, 84, 88,
        109

S

Samuel, Archie Peyton, 16, 68
Samuel, Reuben (stepfather), 16,
    24–25, 67–68

Samuel, Zerelda Cole James
    (mother), 11–12, 14–16, 24–
    25, 68, 93, 95, 97, 101–103
Sheets, John W., 47
Simms, Benjamin, 14, 16
slavery, 13, 16–19, 22, 25, 27,
    30, 36
Ste. Genevieve Savings
    Association robbery, 57–58

T

Thompson, John, 47–48
tourism, 101–104

U

Union Intelligence Service, 54

V

voting rights, 44

W

weapons, 49
Whicher, Joseph, 63–64
William Jewell College, 12, 41
Wymore, George, 41

Y

Younger, Bob, 22, 74, 76, 79,
    80, 103
Younger, Dick, 22
Younger, Henry, 22
Younger, Jim, 22, 68, 79, 80,
    103
Younger, John, 22, 41, 58, 64,
    79
Younger, Thomas Coleman
    "Cole," 22, 32, 33, 41, 42,
    45, 52, 55, 57, 58, 62, 68,
    74, 76, 79, 103
Younger Brothers Capture Event,
    80